BRITISH FAIRY TALES

British FAIRY TALES

RETOLD BY AMABEL WILLIAMS-ELLIS

Illustrated by Pauline Diana Baynes

BLACKIE: GLASGOW AND LONDON

First published 1965
Reprinted 1972
This edition 1976

ISBN 0 216 90290 8 hardback
ISBN 0 216 90230 4 paperback

Blackie and Son Limited
Bishopbriggs, Glasgow G64 2NZ
450/452 Edgware Road, London W2 1EG

Printed in Great Britain by Robert MacLehose & Co. Ltd
Printers to the University of Glasgow

CONTENTS

CONTENTS

BRITISH FAIRY TALES

FIFTY RED NIGHT-CAPS

Once upon a time there was a man who had fifty red night-caps to sell at a fair. His wife put them into a great big sack, and off he went.

Now this happened in a very hot country, and the man's way lay through a big shady wood, so, when he got among the trees, he threw his bag on the ground and down he sat himself to rest. Then, feeling sleepy, he took one of the red night-caps out of his big bag, put it on, lay down and soon went sound asleep.

But there were monkeys in that wood. By and by a great big old monkey came stealing down out of a tree, put out his paw, pulled one of the red night-caps out of the bag, popped it on his head, ran up into his tall tree and sat there grinning and chattering. By and by another monkey came quietly down and he too put his hand into the open bag, seized hold of a red night-cap, put it on, and ran up into another tree. There he sat grinning and chattering. And then another monkey came softly down and took yet another red night-cap, and then another monkey copied him. So, at last, there were forty-nine monkeys in forty-nine red night-caps, all sitting high in the trees chattering and calling out to each other.

They all made such a noise that at last the man woke up, and when he saw nothing but the empty bag in front of him, he was in despair and he cried out:

'Oh, what shall I do! What shall I do! What shall I say to my wife when I take back neither the red night-caps nor the money I was to get for them?' and then, in his misery, he pulled his own red night-cap off his head and threw it on the ground. Whereupon all the forty-nine monkeys, who were watching him, pulled off their forty-nine red night-caps, and threw them down on to the ground as well.

Full of joy the man picked them all up, put them back into the bag, threw the bag over his shoulder, and then off he went and sold them at the fair.

TOM TIT TOT

Once upon a time there was a woman, and she baked five pies, but when they came out of the oven they were dreadful. Slow-baked they were, so that the crust was too hard to bite. So she said to her girl:

'Daughter,' says she, 'you put those there pies on the larder shelf and leave 'em there a little, and they'll come again.' (She meant, you know, that the crust would get soft.) But the girl was that greedy!

'If they'll come again', says she to herself, 'I may as well eat 'em!' And then, would you believe it? The girl set to work and she ate them all—first and last!

Supper-time came and the woman, who'd been hard at work at her spinning, felt hungry and she says to the girl:

'Go you and get one o' them there pies. I dare say they've come again by now.'

The girl went to the larder and she looked, but of course there wasn't anything on the shelf except the five dishes. Back she came to her mother.

'No, Mother! Them pies ain't come again!'

'No one of 'em?' says the mother.

'Not one of 'em,' says the girl.

'Well, come again, or not come again,' says the woman, 'I'll have one for supper.'

'But you can't, Mother! Not if they ain't come again!' says the girl.

'But I can,' says her mother. 'Go and bring the best of 'em.'

'Best or worst,' says the girl, 'I've been and ate them all.'

Well, the woman was so surprised at what her daughter told her that she didn't answer a word. She just took her spinning-wheel to the door, and began to work, and as she span she sang:

'My darter have ate five, five pies today!
My darter have ate five, five pies today!'

Now just then the King came riding down the street and he heard her singing, but what the words might be he couldn't hear, so he stopped and he said:

'What are you a-singing of, my good woman?'

Now she felt ashamed to let the King know what a greedy girl her daughter had been, so she sang him different words:

'My darter have spun five, five skeins today,
My darter have spun five, five skeins today.'

'Stars o' mine!' said the King. 'I never heard tell of any girl that could do that!' Then sitting there on his horse, he thought for a bit and at last he said:

'I want a wife, and I'll marry your daughter. But mind,' says he, 'there'll be a bargain! Eleven months out of the year she shall have all the vittles she likes to eat, and all the gowns she likes to wear, and all the company she likes to keep; but in the last month of the year she'll have to spin five skeins every day. If she doesn't, it'll be off with her head.'

The woman thought a bit.

'Done!' says she at last, and the girl gave her word as well, for of course they both thought what a grand marriage that would be. As for spinning five skeins every day, why, when the time came there'd surely be plenty of ways of getting out of that.

'Likeliest by then the King'll have forgotten all about it,' thinks the mother.

So they were married. Sure enough, for eleven months everything went well. The girl had all the vittles she liked to eat and all the gowns she liked to wear, and all the company she liked to keep.

But when the eleven months were nearly up, she began to think about those five skeins now and again, and to wonder if the King still had them in mind. However, he didn't say a word about them, and of course neither did she.

'Likeliest he's forgot all about 'em,' thinks the girl.

However, the evening of the last day came, and what do you think the King did? He took her to a room in the castle that she'd never set eyes on before. There wasn't anything in it except a spinning-wheel, a stool, and a little narrow bed. Then the King said:

'Here you are, my dear! You'll be shut up in this room tomorrow with some vittles and some flax, and if you haven't spun five skeins by the night, your head'll have to go off.' And with that, away he went about his business.

Well, the girl was fairly frightened out of her life! You see she'd always been such a careless, idle, gatless girl, that she didn't know how to spin at all—let alone how to spin five skeins all in one day. So now what was she going to do next day, when she was to be shut in that room with no one to come nigh nor near to help her? She sat down on a stool in the kitchen, and lor! how she did cry!

All of a sudden she heard a sort of knocking—low down on the kitchen door it was. She upped and she opened the door, and what should she see outside but a little black thing. Like a little old man it was, only that it had a long tail. That queer little thing looked up at her out of its squint eyes and said:

'What are you a-cryin' for?'

'What's that to you?' says the girl.

'Never you mind,' it said. 'Just you tell me what you're a-cryin' for.'

'T'wouldn't do no good if I did tell you,' says she.

'How do you know if it wouldn't?' it said, and as it spoke it twirled its long tail.

'Well,' says the girl, 'I suppose t'wouldn't do no harm to tell even if it didn't do no good.'

So with that she told the little black thing the whole tale, first and last—all about the pies, and the skeins, and the King, and what she and her mother had thought, and what the King had said, and that horrid empty room, and everything.

When she'd done telling, the little thing thought for a while and then it said:

'This is what I'll do. I'll come to the window of that room every morning, and I'll take away the flax and I'll bring it back—all spun—every night.'

Well, now it was the girl's turn to think. 'What's your pay?' says she.

That little black thing looked out of the corners of its squinty eyes and said:

'Pay? Oh, nothing much! I'll just give you three guesses every night to find out my name, and then, if you haven't guessed it afore the month's up, you'll be mine!'

'Done!' says she—you see she felt sure she'd be able to guess its name.

'All right!' says that black impet, and lawks! how it twirled its tail! There wasn't another word between them, and before she could think, the little thing was gone.

Next day—sure enough—the King took her into the empty room that he'd shown her before, and there was nothing in it except the spinning-wheel, the flax, and the stool, and the narrow bed, and the day's vittles.

'There you are!' says the King. 'And if that flax isn't

spun up this night, off goes your head!' And with that he went out and locked the door behind him.

He'd hardly gone, when what should the girl hear but a knocking. It wasn't at the door this time, it was low down on the window.

She upped and she opened it, and there was that little black thing standing on the window-ledge.

'Where's the flax?' it says in its sharp little voice.

'Here it is,' says she. And she handed it out.

Well there the girl sat and did nothing all day long except eat up the vittles. Come evening, the knocking came again at the window. The girl upped and she opened it, and there was that little black thing, and sure enough it had five skeins of beautiful spun flax over its arm.

'Here's the work! Now, what's my name?' it says.

'Is it Bill?' says she.

'No, it ain't,' it says. And it twirled its tail.

'Is it Ned?' says she.

'No, it ain't,' it says. And it twirled its tail harder.

'Is it Mark?' says she.

'No, it ain't,' it says. And it grinned and twirled its tail still faster, and flew away out of the window.

When the King came in, a bit later, there were the five skeins well spun and all ready for him.

'I see I shan't have to have your head off tonight, my dear,' says he. 'You'll have your vittles and your flax in the morning as before,' and with that away he goes.

Well, so it went on. Every day the flax and the vittles were brought to the girl, and every day the little black impet used to come, mornings and evenings. And all day the girl would sit trying to think of names to say when it came at night. But try as she would, she never seemed to hit on the right one.

As it got on towards the end of the month, the impet began to look very maliceful and pleased with itself, and twirled its tail faster and faster.

At last it came to the last day, except one. That impet came at night as usual with the five skeins, and it grinned and said:

'What, my dear? Haven't you got my name yet? '

'Is it Nicodemus?' says she.

'No, t'ain't,' it says.

'Is it Samuel?' says she.

'No, t'ain't,' it says.

'A-well, is it Methusalem?' says she.

'No! T'ain't that neither,' it says.

Then it looks at her with eyes like coals of fire, an' says:

'Woman! There's only tomorrow night left, and THEN YOU'LL BE MINE!' And away it flew.

As you can guess, the girl felt real horrid! However, it wasn't long before she heard the King coming along the passage. In he came, and when he saw the five skeins, he says to her:

'Well, my dear, I don't see but what you'll have your skeins ready tomorrow as well, just like the other nights, and I reckon I shan't have your head cut off, so I'll have supper in here with you tonight!'

So supper was brought for the two of them and another stool for the King, and down they sat.

Now the King hadn't eaten but a mouthful or so, when he stops and begins to laugh.

'What is it?' says she.

'A-why,' says he, 'I was out hunting today, and I came to a place in the wood I'd never seen before. There was an old chalk-pit among the trees. And it seemed to me that I could hear a sort of a humming. So I got off my horse, and I crept right quiet to the edge of that chalk-pit, and I looked down. What should I see but the funniest little black thing you ever set eyes on. And what that thing was a-doing you'll never guess! It had a little spinning-wheel, and it was a-spinning wonderful fast, and as it spun it kept on twirling its tail and singing.'

'What words did it sing?' asked the girl softly, trying to keep very quiet.

'The funniest words!' said the King. 'Over and over it sang them, like this:

" *Ninny ninny not,*
My name's Tom-Tit-Tot " '

When the girl heard this, she could have jumped out of her skin for joy, but she didn't say a word about it to the King, no, not though they talked quite friendly like all the rest of the evening.

Next morning, when it came for the flax, that black little thing looked more maliceful than ever! And in the evening that impet knocked hard at the window-pane—ever so much bolder!

The girl opened the window, and this time that thing didn't stay out on the ledge, but came right in, right down on to the floor of the room. It was grinning from ear to ear, and its tail was twirling round so fast!

'What's my name?' it says, as it gave her the skeins.

'Is that Solomon?' says she, pretending to be frightened.

'No, t'ain't!' it says, and that impet came a bit nearer to her.

'Well—is that Zebedee?' says she again.

'No, t'ain't!' says the impet. And that little black thing laughed and twirled its tail till you couldn't hardly see it! 'Take time, woman!' it says. 'Take time, remember! NEXT GUESS AND YOU'RE MINE!' And it stretched out its horrid black hands at her.

But with that the girl stepped back a pace or two, and then she looked that black impet in the eye and she laughed out loud, and she pointed her finger at it, and she called out:

'NINNY NINNY NOT,
YOUR NAME'S TOM-TIT-TOT!'

When it heard her say the words, it shrieked most horribly. But a bargain's a bargain, so away it had to fly into the dark, and she never saw it again.

THE WEE, WEE MANNIE

Once upon a time, in Scotland it was, there was a wee, wee Mannie, and his mother had a big, big cow.

Out he went to milk her one morning, and when he was close up to the big, big cow he said to her:

'Hold still, my Coo, my hinny,
Hold still, my hinny, my Coo,
And ye shall have for your dinner
What but a milk white doo.'

(He meant a 'dove' you know.) But the big, big cow didn't want a dove for her dinner, and she wouldn't hold still.

'Hoots!' said the wee, wee Mannie:

'Hold still, my Coo, my dearie,
And fill my bucket wi'-milk,
And if ye'll be no contrairy
I'll gi'e ye a gown o' silk.'

But the big, big cow wouldn't hold still.

'Look at that, now!' said the wee, wee Mannie:

'Now what's a wee, wee mannie to do,
Wi' such a great contrairy coo?'

So off he went, back to his mother at the house.

'Mother,' says he, 'Coo won't stand still, so wee, wee Mannie can't milk big, big Coo!'

'Hoots!' says his mother. 'Take a stick and beat the Coo.'

So off went the wee, wee Mannie to get a stick from the tree, and he said to the tree:

'Break, stick, break,
And I'll give ye a cake.'

But the stick wouldn't break, so back he went to the house.

'Mother,' says he, 'Coo won't hold still, stick won't break, wee, wee Mannie can't beat big, big Coo.'

'Hoots!' says his mother. 'Go to the butcher and bid him kill Coo.'

So off he went to the butcher, and he said:

'Butcher, kill the big, big Coo,
She'll give us no more milk the noo.'

But the Butcher wouldn't

kill the cow unless he was paid a silver penny, so back the Mannie went to the house.

'Mother,' says he 'Coo won't hold still, stick won't break, Butcher won't kill her without he gets a silver penny, and so wee, wee Mannie *still* can't milk big, big Coo.'

'Well', said his mother, 'go to the Coo and tell her there's a weary, weary lady with long yellow hair that's weeping for a cup o' milk.'

So off he went and told the Coo, but she wouldn't hold still, so back he went and told his mother.

'Well,' said she, 'tell the Coo there's a fine, fine laddie from the wars sitting by the weary, weary lady with the long golden hair, and she weeping for a cup o' milk.'

So off he went and told the Coo, but she wouldn't hold still, so back he went to his mother.

'Hoots!' said his mother. 'Tell the big, big Coo there's

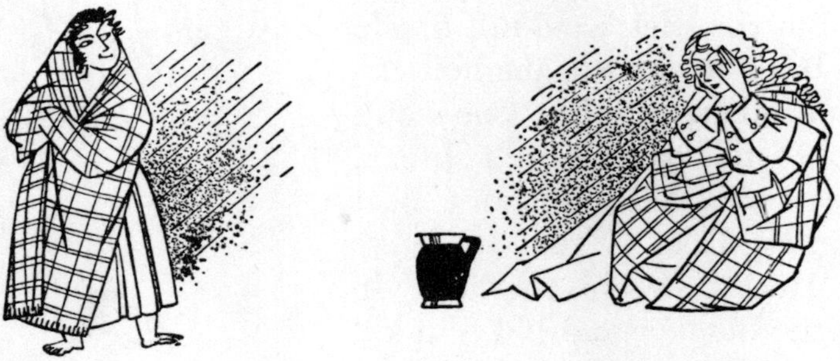

a sharp, sharp sword at the belt of the fine, fine laddie from the wars who sits beside the weary, weary lady with the long golden hair, and she weeping for a cup o' milk.'

And he told the big, big Coo, but she wouldn't hold still.

Then said his mother:

'Run quick and tell the big, big Coo that her head's going to be cut off by the sharp, sharp sword in the hands of the fine, fine laddie, if she doesn't give the cup o' milk that the weary, weary lady is weeping for.'

Then the wee, wee Mannie went off and told the big, big Coo, and it was all true!

So when the cow saw the glint of the sharp, sharp sword in the hand of the fine, fine laddie come from the wars, that was with the weary, weary lady that was weeping for a cup of milk, she reckoned she'd better hold still.

So, at last, the wee, wee Mannie was able to milk the big, big Coo and the weary, weary lady with the long golden hair hushed her weeping as soon as she got her cup o' milk. When he saw that, the fine, fine laddie, new come from the wars, put by his sharp, sharp sword, and after that, all went well that didn't go ill.

THE KING, THE SAINT, AND THE GOOSE

Did you ever hear what happened to good King O'Toole, who lived long ago in Ireland, and how it was that his old age was made pleasant to him?

If you never heard it, isn't it high time you did?

Now in his young days, King O'Toole had been one of the finest young fellows in all Ireland. He loved hunting better than anything in the world, and from the rising of the sun till darkness came he would be out galloping and hallooing with his horse and his hounds.

This went on merrily for a long while, but in the end the King grew too old and stiff to be hunting all day, summer and winter, be it wet or be it fine. Indeed a winter came when it was as much as the poor old king could do to hobble about with a stick or even a crutch. Why, then it's lost he was, for he felt as if there wasn't any amusement or diversion left for him in the world.

So at last, what did that poor old King do, but get himself a goose to amuse and divert him. You may laugh, but she was a very good faithful creature was that goose.

For a while they had a lot of pleasure together, her

and King O'Toole. She would fly round and about, but would always come back when he called her and would waddle after him if that was what would please him. On a Friday (that, you know, is a Fast day) she would swim far out into the lake two or three times, and come back each time to him with a nice plump trout for his dinner.

So that good creature was all poor old King O'Toole's amusement and pleasure. But my dear! The sadness of the world! The time came when the poor goose grew old too, and one winter the truth was that she was as stiff in the wing as her master was in the leg, so that, try as she would, the poor faithful creature couldn't amuse him any more. Why then, the old King was lost entirely and had no more pleasure in life.

One day these two distressful creatures were sitting by the side of the lake. The King had his poor old goose in his arms, and he was looking down fondly at her, the tears in his eyes, lamenting because neither he nor she had any more pleasure. Then presently he let her go and she waddled off, to get a bite to eat. But the old King sat on, thinking that he might as well be dead and drowned in the lake, as live such a miserable distressful life.

Then he happened to look up, and what should he see standing before him but a decent young fellow that seemed to be a stranger to those parts.

'God save you, King O'Toole,' said the decent young fellow.

'How come you to know my name?' says the King.

'Never mind for that!' answers the fellow. 'I know a lot of what passes. And may I make bold to ask how is your goose, King O'Toole?'

'And how come you to know about my goose?' asked

the King (for you see she was out of sight now, among the weeds.)

'I know all about her. No matter how,' said the young fellow, smiling.

'And who may you be?' asked the King.

'An honest man,' answered the fellow.

'And how do you get a living?' asked the King.

'By making old things as good as new.'

'Is it a tinker you are then?' asked the King.

'No. I've got a better trade than that. What would you say, King O'Toole, if I was to offer to make your old goose as good as new?'

'As good as new?' asked the King, and he smiled all over his poor old face, thinking that, of all the pleasures of this world, that would please him the best.

'Yes! As good as new,' said the young fellow, nodding.

King O'Toole gave a whistle, and out of the reeds came his poor old goose, waddling and limping. As obedient as a hound she was, that creature, and faithful to her poor old crippled master. When the young man looked down and saw her he nodded again.

'Yes,' says he, 'I could do the job for you easy enough.'

'By the holy word,' says the King, looking down in his turn and seeing the poor old bag-of-bones of a goose, 'if you can do that, why you're the cleverest young fellow in seven parishes!'

'I'm better than that, bedad,' says the young man, laughing, 'but what will you give me now, if I do the job for you?'

'I'll give you whatever you ask for,' says the King. 'Isn't that fair enough?'

'Will you give me all the ground the goose covers the first time she flies after she's been made as good as new?'

'Indeed I will,' says the King.

'You'll not go back on your word?' says the young fellow.

'I will not,' says the King.

Then the young man called to the poor bag-of-bones of a goose:

'You poor unhappy old cripple!' says he, catching her gently by the wings. 'It's I that will make you the fine sporting bird again!' With that he made the sign of the Cross over her and then he threw her up into the air and, as he threw her, he blew at her feathers just to give her a bit of a lift. Sakes alive! If that goose didn't fly off from his hand as if it was one of the eagles of the mountains that she was. Aye, and she sported and capered in the air with delight, just like any swallow.

It was a beautiful sight to see the old King, for he was there with his mouth open for joy and surprise, looking at his poor old goose, and she flying as light as a lark in the sky.

Well, she had a good fly round—out of sight and back again—and then she lit down at her master's feet with a shake of her wings, and when he had patted her head and stroked her all down her back he could tell that she was as good, and even better, than ever she had been.

'Sure, you're the darling of the world,' says the King to the goose.

'And what do you say to me?' asked the young fellow.

'I say you're the cleverest fellow that walks the ground of Ireland,' replied the King, still looking at his goose.

'No more than that?'

'I say I'll be grateful to you to my dying day.'

'But will you do as you said and give me the land that the goose flew over just now?'

'I will,' said the King, looking up at last. 'You'd be welcome to it if it was the last acre I'd got.'

'You're a good, decent old man, for you keep to a bargain,' says the young fellow, 'and well for you and your goose that you are, else your bird would never fly again!'

'But who are you?' asked the King for the second time that morning, for he seemed to see a change coming over the young fellow.

'I'm St. Kevin,' he answered.

'Oh, Queen of Heaven!' said the King, making the sign of the Cross, and dropping on his knees as well as he

could for the stiffness of his joints. 'And is it with a holy saint I've been speaking and discoursing all this while?'

'It is,' said St. Kevin.

'And me thinking it was only a decent young lad!'

'I came in disguise,' said the saint, 'so how would you be knowing with whom you were talking and discoursing? I came to try you, King O'Toole, and I've been finding this morning that you're a decent old King, for it seems that you'll keep a bargain even with one you took to be no more than a tinker.'

Well, King O'Toole had kept his bargain, so sure enough he had his goose as good as new to amuse and divert him till the day he died, and though 'twas only a little bit of a kingdom that he had left, the saint evermore provided for the two of them—for the King and the goose.

So now you know how it came about that all that queer-shaped bit of ground in that part of Ireland belongs to one of the saints of Heaven.

TEENY-TINY

Once upon a time there was a teeny tiny woman who lived all alone in a teeny tiny house. One evening this teeny tiny woman put on her teeny tiny bonnet and thought to her teeny tiny self that she would take a teeny tiny walk. Now when this teeny tiny woman had only gone a teeny tiny way she came to a teeny tiny gate, and this teeny tiny gate led into a teeny tiny field. So she went through this teeny tiny gate and began to walk a teeny tiny way along beside the teeny tiny hedge of this teeny tiny field. After a teeny tiny time, what should she see but a teeny tiny bone. When she saw that she thought to her teeny tiny self:

'This teeny tiny bone would be just right for my teeny tiny supper.'

So the teeny tiny woman didn't walk even a teeny tiny bit farther, but just picked up the teeny tiny bone, put it into her teeny tiny pocket, and went back through the teeny tiny gate to her own teeny tiny house.

Now when this teeny tiny woman got home she felt a teeny tiny bit tired, so instead of making her teeny tiny supper, she put the teeny tiny bone into her teeny tiny cupboard and she went straight off to her teeny tiny bed.

But she had only been asleep in her teeny tiny bed for a teeny tiny time when she woke up, and she thought that she could hear a teeny tiny voice which seemed to come from her teeny tiny cupboard, and she thought that what the teeny tiny voice said was:

'Give me my bone!'

And this teeny tiny woman was a teeny tiny bit frightened, so she hid her teeny tiny head under the teeny tiny bedclothes and went to sleep again. And when she had been to sleep again for a teeny tiny time, the teeny tiny voice again cried out a teeny tiny bit louder:

'Give me my bone!'

This made the teeny tiny woman a teeny tiny bit more frightened, so she hid her teeny tiny head a teeny tiny bit farther under the teeny tiny bedclothes. And when the teeny tiny woman had been to sleep again for a teeny tiny time, the teeny tiny voice from the teeny tiny cupboard said again a teeny tiny bit louder:

'Give me my bone!'

At this the teeny tiny woman was a teeny tiny bit more frightened, but she put her teeny tiny head out from the teeny tiny bedclothes, and said in her loudest teeny tiny voice:

'TAKE IT!'

HAPPY BOZ'LL

Once upon a time there was a gipsy, and his name was Happy Boz'll, and he had a knife-grinding barrow and a donkey, and he used to put his wife and child on the top of the barrow and away they'd go along the road. But, in the end, he cut up the barrow and made tent-poles out of it, and he and his wife began to live in his new tent.

Well, one day his donkey went away, and he didn't know where it had got to. So after a bit, he said what he'd said fifty times before (only not in that exact spot, as you might say).

'Bless my soul,' said he, 'wherever has that donkey got to?'

Now there was a tree close by, and a voice from the tree called out:

'I'm here, my Happy! Getting you a bundle of sticks to make you a fire.'

And when he looked, he saw that it was his own donkey that was up the tree! Well, the donkey came down with a lot of sticks—he'd been up there for a week, you see, getting firewood.

Now Happy had a dog, and they went out one day to see what they could get for the pot. Happy went down one side of the hedge and the dog went down the other. They put up two hares and the dog ran after them both. He was racing across the field like mad when, would you believe it, he cut himself right through with a scythe that had been left out among the grass. Well, that was fine, for as you can see, now one half-dog could run after one hare and the other half-dog could run after the other. What happened was that the two half-dogs caught the two hares, and then the two halves smacked together again, and the dog said:

'Well, I've got 'em, my Happy!' But you see that couldn't go on, so after a while the dog died.

Well, Happy was sorry to lose his dog, but it happened that he had a hole in the knee of his breeches, so he cut off a piece of the dead dog's skin to mend it with. And that day twelvemonth his breeches knee burst open and barked at him.

And that's the end of this tale about Happy Boz'll.

JOHNNY-CAKE

Once upon a time an old man and old woman lived in a little house. One morning the old woman got up and she made a Johnny-Cake (that's a Journey Cake, you know). She put it in the pan and she put the pan on the fire. Then she said to the old man:

'I'm going out to milk the cow. Do you turn the Johnny-Cake as soon as it's done on one side.'

Now the old man was lazy, so, instead of getting up, he lay abed, and by-and-by he said to himself:

'Oh dear, I suppose I shall soon have to get up and turn that Johnny-Cake!'

'I can turn myself!' called out a voice from the fire-place.

The old man was so surprised that, at first, he couldn't move, no, not even when he saw the Johnny-Cake jump out of the pan. Then, when he *did* get out of bed, the Johnny-Cake was too quick for him and, in a moment, it was through the door, and out down the garden path, rolling and hopping end-over-end. The old man shouted and hollered like mad:

'Stop, you Johnny-Cake! Stop, you Johnny-Cake!' and he made such shouting that the old woman left off milking the cow and ran to see what was the matter. When she saw what was going on, she set down the milk-pail and ran after the Johnny-Cake. But bless you, run as they would, they couldn't catch him! That Johnny-Cake outran them both.

By and by they were so out of breath that they had to sit down and rest, with Johnny-Cake far away down the road.

On ran Johnny-Cake, and by and by he came to two well-diggers and when they saw what it was coming down the road they looked up from their work and they called out:

'Where are ye going, Johnny-Cake?'

Johnny-Cake shouted back:

'I've outrun an old man and an old woman, and I can outrun you too-o-o!'

'Oh you can, can you? We'll see about that!' said they, and they threw down their picks and shovels and ran after him; but it was no use, they couldn't catch up with him, and soon they too had to sit down by the roadside to rest.

On ran Johnny-Cake, and by and by he came to two ditch-diggers who were at their work.

'Where are you going, Johnny-Cake?' they called out, and as he ran by Johnny-Cake shouted back:

'I've outrun an old man and an old woman, and two well-diggers, and I can outrun you too-o-o!'

'Oh, you can, can you? We'll see about that!' cried the ditch-diggers and, throwing down their spades, they ran after him. But Johnny-Cake soon outstripped them, and seeing they could never catch him, they gave up the chase and sat down to rest.

On went Johnny-Cake, and by and by he came to a bear. The bear said:

'Where are ye going, Johnny-Cake?'

He said:

'I've outrun an old man and an old woman, and two well-diggers, and two ditch-diggers, and I can outrun you too-o-o!'

'Oh you can, can you?' growled the bear. 'We'll see

about that!' and the bear got up and lumbered along as fast as his legs could carry him after Johnny-Cake, who never even stopped to look behind him.

Before long the bear was left so far behind that he saw he might as well give up the hunt first as last, so he stretched himself out by the roadside to rest.

On went Johnny-Cake, and by and by he came to a wolf. The wolf called out:

'Where are you going, Johnny-Cake?'

Johnny-Cake shouted back:

'I've outrun an old man and an old woman, and two

well-diggers, and two ditch-diggers, and a bear, and I can outrun you too-o-o!'

'Oh you can, can you?' snarled the wolf. 'We'll see about that!' and he set off at a gallop after Johnny-Cake. But Johnny-Cake just went on and on, so fast that the wolf soon saw there was no hope of catching him, and lay down to rest.

On went Johnny-Cake, and by and by he came to a fox that lay quietly in a corner of the fence. The fox called out to him in a sharp voice, but without getting up:

'Where are you going, Johnny-Cake?'

Johnny-Cake shouted back:

'I've outrun an old man and an old woman, and two well-diggers, and two ditch-diggers, and a bear, and a wolf, and I can outrun you too-o-o!'

'I can't quite hear you, Johnny-Cake,' said the fox softly. 'Won't you come just a *leetle* closer?' and with that the fox pricked his ears and turned his head to one side.

Then for the first time Johnny-Cake stopped his race, and he did go a little closer, and he called out in a very loud voice:

'I'VE OUTRUN AN OLD MAN, AND AN OLD WOMAN, AND TWO WELL-DIGGERS, AND TWO DITCH-DIGGERS, AND A BEAR, AND A WOLF, AND I CAN OUTRUN YOU TOO-O-O!'

'I still can't quite hear you, Johnny-Cake! Won't you come a *leetle* closer?' said the fox in a weak voice, and as he spoke he stretched out his neck towards Johnny-Cake, and put one paw behind his ear.

Johnny-Cake came up quite close this time, and leaning towards the fox, he screamed out louder than before:

'I'VE OUTRUN AN OLD MAN, AND AN OLD WOMAN, AND TWO WELL-DIGGERS, AND TWO DITCH-DIGGERS, AND A BEAR, AND A WOLF AND I CAN OUTRUN YOU TOO-O-O!'

'Oh you can, can you?' yelped the fox, and with that he snapped up Mr. Johnny-Cake in the twinkling of an eye.

THE THREE LITTLE PIGS

Once upon a time there lived an old sow with three little pigs, and as she hadn't got enough to keep them, she sent them out into the world to seek their fortunes.

The first little pig met a man with a cartload of straw, and said to him:

'Man, man, give me that straw to build me a house.'

So the man did, and the little pig built himself a house. Presently along came the wolf, and knocked at the door, and said:

'Little pig, little pig, let me come in.'

To which the pig answered:

'No, no, by the hair on my chinny chin chin!'

'Then I'll huff, and I'll puff, and I'll blow your house in,' said the Wolf.

So he huffed, and he puffed, and at last he blew the house in, and ate up the little pig.

The second little pig met a man with a bundle of furze, and said to him:

'Man, man, give me that furze to build me a house.'

So the man did, and the little pig built himself a house.

Along came the wolf, and said:

'Little pig, little pig, let me come in!'

'No, no, by the hair on my chinny chin chin!'

'Then I'll puff, and I'll huff, and I'll blow your house in,' said the Wolf.

So he huffed, and he puffed, and he puffed, and he huffed, and at last he blew the house in, and ate up the little pig.

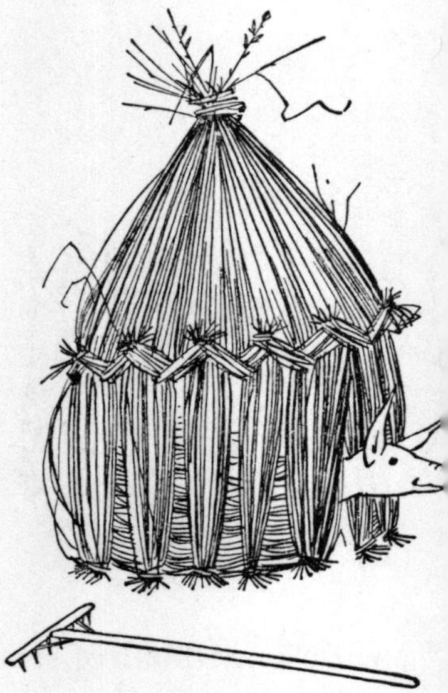

The third little pig met a man with a cartload of bricks, and said to him:

'Man, man, give me those bricks to build me a house.'

So the man gave him the bricks, and the little pig built himself a house with them.

Soon the wolf came just as he had to the other little pigs.

'Little pig, little pig, let me come in!', said the Wolf.

'No, no, by the hair on my chinny chin chin!'

'Then I'll huff, and I'll puff, and I'll blow your house in.'

Well, he huffed, and he puffed, and he huffed and he

puffed, and he huffed and he puffed; but he could *not* blow the house in. When he found that he couldn't blow the house down with all his huffing and puffing, the Wolf said:

'Little pig! I know where there is a nice field of turnips.'

'Where?' said the little pig.

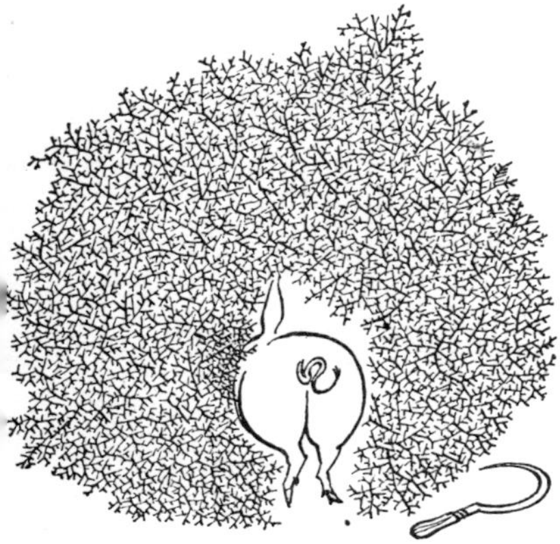

'Oh, in Mr. Smith's Home-field, and if you'll be ready tomorrow morning I'll call for you, and we will go together, and get some turnips for dinner.'

'Very well', said the little pig, 'I'll be ready. What time do you mean to go?'

'At six o'clock.'

Well, the little pig got up at five, and got the turnips before the wolf came (which he did about six).

The wolf said:

'Little pig, are you ready?'

The little pig said:

'Ready! I've been and come back again, and got a nice potful of turnips for dinner.'

The wolf felt angry at this, but he thought that he

would be up to the little pig somehow or other, so he said:

'Little pig! I know where there is a nice apple-tree.'

'Where?' said the pig.

'Down at Merry-garden,' answered the wolf, 'and if you won't deceive me I'll come for you, at five o'clock tomorrow and we'll get some apples.'

Well, the little pig bustled up the next morning at four o'clock, and off he went for the apples, hoping to get back before the Wolf came; but this time he had farther to go, and he had to climb the tree as well, so that, just as he was coming down from it, he saw the Wolf coming, which, as you may suppose, frightened him very much.

The Wolf came up and saw him and said:

'Little pig! What! Are you here before me? Are they nice apples?'

'Yes, very nice,' said the little pig. 'I'll throw you down one.'

And he threw the apple so far, that, while the Wolf was gone to pick it up, the little pig had time to jump down out of the tree and run home.

The next day the Wolf came again, and said to the little pig:

'Little pig! There is a fair at Shanklin this afternoon, will you go?'

'Oh yes,' said the pig, 'I'll go; what time will you be ready?'

'At three,' said the Wolf.

But once more the little pig went off before the time and got to the fair, bought a butter-churn and was going home with it when he saw the wolf coming. Then the little pig felt frightened. So he got into the churn to hide, and as he climbed in he set it rolling so that the butter-churn rolled down the hill with the pig in it. This frightened the Wolf so much, that he ran home without ever getting to the fair. Instead he went to the little pig's house, and told him how frightened he had been by a great round thing which came rolling over and over down the hill past him. Then the little pig said:

'Hah, I frightened you, then! I'd been to the fair and bought a butter-churn, and when I saw you, I got into it. That was *me*, rolling down the hill!'

Then the wolf was very angry indeed, and declared he *would* eat the little pig, and decided that the best way would be to get down the chimney after him. When the little pig saw what the Wolf was doing, he made up a blazing fire, hung a pot full of water over it, and, just as the Wolf was coming down the chimney, he took off the lid of the pot, and in fell the Wolf. Then the little pig put on the lid again in an instant, boiled up the Wolf, ate him for supper, and lived happy ever afterwards.

THE CHANGELING

Long, long ago, a man and his wife lived in a little cottage. They had one son who was born not so long after they were married, and then, a long while after, another baby was born to them, and soon, times being bad, the elder son went for a soldier and off to the wars.

Well, the woman was sorry to see him go, but she was pleased with her baby which was as nice and as rosy, and as contented a little boy as you could wish to see.

But when this baby was about six months old, things began to go wrong. Not only did her good man take ill and die, but the baby didn't seem to thrive any more. It seemed quite changed and it cried and fretted day and night, and though it ate and drank enough for two, it didn't grow or fatten, and instead it seemed to get skinnier and skinnier and yellower and yellower.

Well the woman tried to do her duty by it and to make a living as best she could, by taking in washing and such-like, and she tried, as well, to get word to her elder son to come back and help her. But, being away at the wars, he never got the message. So, what with a baby that cried and fretted and looked yellow and didn't grow, and that ate enough for a grown man, and what with being so poor, the woman had a sad life of it.

At last, when seven years had gone by, there came one day a loud knock at the door, and when she opened it she saw that a handsome young soldier waited in the porch. She stood for a moment without saying a word, so that the soldier was the first to make a move, and what should he do but take her in his arms and kiss her.

'Don't you know me, Mother!' says he, and indeed the fact is that, for a moment, she hadn't known him. He'd grown so tall, and he was so handsome, that it had seemed too good to be true that this strong young fellow should be her own son.

Well, it seemed that he'd heard from the neighbours the bad news that his father was dead, but he hadn't heard a word about his brother, so he looked round, expecting to see a little lad pop out from somewhere.

'Where's the little 'un, Mother?' asks he presently, and with that she heaved a sigh and shook her head.

'Not dead?' asks the soldier.

'No, not dead,' says she. 'He's just started again, can't you hear him?'

So the soldier listened, and sure enough, he could hear a kind of a peevish sort of a whimpering with a shrill weak kind of a shriek to it, and this noise came from the cradle in the corner. So he went to look closer, and he drew back the quilt and there lay a little shrivelled-up yellow thing with the squintiest black eyes that ever you saw.

'How's this?' asked the soldier.

'Can't talk, can't walk, and eats as much as a man!' said the mother sorrowfully. 'Seven years he's lain in that cradle and as fractious and hungry as can be. What's the matter, and how to make him thrive, and what to do with him, I don't know I'm sure!' and with that she burst out crying.

Well, the soldier put his hand on her arm to comfort her, but he kept on looking down at the cradle, and he didn't answer for a minute or two. At last he said:

'What'll you be doing tomorrow, Mother?'

'It's the day for me to go and collect the clothes for washing,' says she, 'but I shan't be long gone.'

'You stop out all morning, Mother, have a chat with the neighbours and enjoy yourself a bit,' says the soldier, 'and I'll take a turn minding him,' and he pointed at what was in the cradle.

Well, at first she wouldn't agree, but it was so long since she'd had even a minute to be a bit sociable, that when the next morning came fine and sunny, she said she would, and she told her big son just what to do for the fractious thing, and off she went.

The soldier started off all right and he fed the baby when it yelled, just as his mother had said. But after that he went out and looked about a bit outside the house. When he came back he'd got a few things in his hand. You wouldn't ever guess what they were. They were an empty eggshell, a few grains of barley, and just one flower off a hop-vine. He set these things down on the kitchen table and then, seeing that the fire had gone a bit low, he sat down to blow it up with the bellows.

The little yellow thing wasn't crying or whimpering for once, and as the soldier got up to go outside again for a drop of water, he was well pleased to see that it was watching every move he made—watching out of its little black bad-tempered squinty eyes.

When the soldier came back into the room he left the

door open—seeming to do this quite by chance. He could see that the thing was still watching him. Then, very carefully, he began pouring a little of the water into the eggshell, and then made out to be very busy putting the grain or two of barley and the hop-flower into the eggshell as well. He was well pleased when he saw, over his shoulder, that the thing was fairly sitting up in the cradle so as to see better. The soldier pretended to take no notice, of course, but went on busily with what he was doing. And now he was taking the eggshell very carefully in his mother's tongs and holding it over the fire. Then he had another look over his shoulder and he saw that the thing wasn't only sitting up, it was out of the cradle and standing there on the floor, so as to see better. You never saw anything look so surprised as that little squinty thing looked! Still, the soldier made out that he hadn't noticed anything.

At last the water in the eggshell began to boil, and then the thing could bear it no longer, and the soldier heard it say:

'I'm old! I'm old! I'm ever so old! But never before did I see a soldier brewing beer in an eggshell.'

'So you're old, are you?' said the soldier. 'And you can talk, can you! Then you can run as well!' and with that he sprang up from the fire with the tongs in his hand, and he chased that little squinty thing all round the kitchen, and then out through the door, and down the garden, and over two fields, and then, at last, it vanished.

But when the soldier got back to the house there he found a handsome little rosy lad of seven years, standing in the porch. The soldier quickly picked up the boy in his arms, carried him over the threshold, and brought him in. For he knew, of course, that this was his own true brother, who must have been all these years with the fairies who had put the squinty-eyed, bad-natured changeling in his place.

You can guess how surprised and delighted his mother was when she came back and saw her own child again.

Well, it wasn't long before the soldier got work near-by, and could earn a decent living for them, so that the mother didn't have to take in washing any more, and so the three of them lived happy for many a long year.

But the queer part of it all was that, ask as they would, the little lad was never able to tell them anything about his life with the fairies or about how they had reared him. Only he knew well enough that the woman was his own mother, and that it was the soldier who was his brother and who had broken the spell and brought him home.

KATE CRACKERNUTS

Once there was a king and a queen, as many a one has been.

The King had a daughter called Anne, and the Queen had one called Kate, and though Anne was far bonnier than the Queen's daughter, there was no jealousy between them and they loved one another like real sisters. It was the Queen that was jealous of the King's daughter, and she cast about how to spoil her beauty. She went to ask the henwife, and the henwife told her to send the lassie to her next morning, but said the henwife:

'She must come, fasting.'

So early next morning, the Queen said to Anne:

'Go, my dear, to the henwife in the glen, and get some fresh eggs.' So Anne took a basket, but as she passed on her way through the kitchen she happened to see a crust, and she picked it up, to eat as she went along.

When she came to the henwife's she asked for eggs, as she had been told to do, and the henwife said to her:

'Lift the lid off that crock there and see.'

The lassie did so, but nothing happened.

'Go home to your Mammie and tell her to keep her larder door better locked,' said the henwife.

So the girl went home and told the Queen what the henwife had said. The Queen knew from this that the lassie had had something to eat, so she watched the next morning to make sure that she went away fasting. But the Princess saw some country folk picking peas by the roadside and she passed the time of day with them, and as they talked together she took a pod or so, and ate the peas as she walked.

When she came to the henwife's, she asked for eggs as before.

'Lift the lid off the crock, and you'll see,' said the henwife.

So Anne lifted the lid, but again, nothing happened.

Then the henwife was rare and angry and she said to Anne:

'Tell your Mammie that the pot won't boil if there's no fire under it.'

So Anne went home and told the Queen what the hen wife had said.

The third day the Queen herself went along with the girl, and this time, when Anne lifted the lid off the

pot, off falls her own pretty head, and on jumps a sheep's head.

So now the jealous Queen was quite satisfied, because Anne wasn't the prettiest any more. But when Kate saw what had happened, she was sorrier than she had ever been in her life. She took a piece of white linen and wrapped it round her sister's head, and they both went away hand in hand to seek their fortunes.

They went along and they went along, till at last they came to a castle. Kate knocked at the door and asked for a night's lodging for herself and a sick sister. They were let in and found that it was a king's castle. It seemed that this King had two sons, and one of them was sickening away to death and no one could find out what ailed him, and the curious thing was no one could ever watch a whole night beside him. Those that tried were never seen again, so now the king had offered a peck of silver to anyone who would try to stop up with him.

Now Kate was a very brave girl, so she up and offered to sit out the night by the Prince's bedside.

Nothing happened till midnight. But as the strokes of twelve rang out from the clock in the castle tower, the sick Prince got up out of his bed, dressed himself, and slipped downstairs. Kate followed. But he walked like one that was still asleep and didn't seem to notice her.

Out of the door of the castle he went and on to the stableyard where his horse stood saddled: he called his hound, jumped into the saddle, and all this as if he were in a dream. Kate, watching her time, leapt lightly up behind him.

Away they rode through the greenwood, and Kate, as they passed, kept picking the nuts that grew on the trees till she had filled her apron with them. They rode on

beyond the wood till they came to a green hill. The horse stopped as if he knew the place, and now for the first time the Prince spoke.

'Open, open, green hill, and let the young Prince in with his horse and his hound,' and Kate quickly added, 'and his lady up behind him.'

Sure enough, the green hill opened for them and they passed in, and the Prince dismounted and Kate slipped down as well. They found themselves in a splendid hall, brightly lighted up. Many beautiful ladies, who seemed to be fairies, crowded round the Prince, and then led him off to the dance.

Nobody seemed to notice Kate, so she was able to hide herself behind the door. She watched for a long time and saw how the Prince danced and danced till he could dance no more and fell almost fainting upon a couch. Then she saw how the fairy ladies fanned him and revived him, till at last he got up and went on dancing.

At last she heard how, outside, a cock crew, and then

she saw how the Prince made all haste to get on his horse again. Once more Kate managed to jump up behind, without being seen, and home they rode.

Next morning his attendants came in and found the Prince lying pale in his bed as usual; but Kate was still there, sitting by the fire, and cracking nuts.

Kate told them that the Prince had had a good night, and that she would sit up another night, if they cared to give her a peck of gold. As Kate was the first that had ever managed to stay the night through, they were willing enough that she should try.

The second night began very much as the first had done. The Prince got up at midnight, but all in a sort of dream. Away he rode once more to the green hill and the fairy ball, and once more Kate went with him, and once more she gathered nuts as they rode through the greenwood. But this time, when she was hidden behind the door again, she didn't watch the Prince, for she felt sure that he would dance, and dance, and dance, till he was faint. This time she looked about her instead, and she noticed how a fairy baby was playing with a wand, and she overheard one of the fairy ladies.

'Three strokes of that wand would make Kate's sick sister as bonnie as ever she was,' said the fairy.

So what did Kate do but roll nuts, and roll nuts, to the fairy baby, till the little thing began to toddle after them and, as it toddled after the nuts, it let fall the wand. Then Kate took up the wand and hid it in her apron. At cockcrow the Prince got on his horse again, and they rode home as before. But this time Kate rushed to the room where Anne was sleeping, and touched her three times with the wand. The moment she had done this, sure enough, the nasty sheep's head fell off, and Anne was her own pretty self again, and you can guess how she kissed and embraced her kind sister Kate.

Now, though the Prince was no better, the King asked Kate if she would watch by him again, but this time she said that she would only agree if she was allowed to marry him if he was cured, and the King said she could.

All went as on the first two nights, except that this time the fairy baby was playing with a little dead bird with pretty coloured feathers. Kate heard one of the fairies say:

'Three bites of that bonnie birdie would make the sick Prince as well as ever he was!'

Again Kate rolled nuts to the fairy baby and rolled nuts, till she had rolled almost all that were in her apron, and at last it toddled after the rolling nuts and dropped the birdie, whereupon Kate picked it up and put it in her apron.

At cockcrow they set off again, and were soon home. But instead of sitting by the fire cracking nuts, Kate began to pluck feathers and blow up the fire, and then she cooked the birdie. Soon there arose a delicious smell, and it was so good that it waked the sick Prince.

'Oh,' said he, 'I wish I had a bite of that birdie!'

So Kate cut off a piece and gave him a bite of the birdie, and when he had eaten it he was able to prop himself up on his elbow. Kate went on with her roasting and by and by he cried out again:

'Oh, if I but had another bite of that birdie!'

So Kate gave him another bite, and with the second bite he was strong enough to sit up in his bed. Then he said again:

'Oh, if I but had a third bite of that birdie!'

So Kate gave him a third bite, and when he had eaten it, he rose up as hale and strong as ever he was, and came and sat down by the fire by Kate. So, when the folk came in next morning, they found Kate and the young Prince quite happy, sitting by the fire and cracking nuts together. Meanwhile the other Prince, his brother, had seen Anne and had fallen in love with her—as indeed everybody did who saw her sweet pretty face.

So the sick son married the well sister, and the well son married the sick sister, and they all

'Lived happy
And died happy,
And never drank
Out of a dry cappy.'

CLEVER OONAGH

There was once a giant in Ireland called Cucullin, and another giant that was also supposed to be a mighty warrior, though he wasn't near so big. His name was Fin.

There's many a terrible tale told about these two—Cucullin and Fin—and their great and famous deeds and their battles. But there's one story about them and about Fin's wife Oonagh which is different. Maybe it's just a tale that was told round about the country by those who were sick and tired of hearing only about their killing and slaughtering and the great deeds. Perhaps a few people wanted to have the laugh of them.

Now Fin had his house at the very top of a steep hill called Knockmany, which wasn't really just such a very convenient place for a house, because, you see, whichever way the wind blew, it always blew up there. Another thing was that, when her husband Fin was away, Oonagh had always to go down to the very bottom of the steep hill to the spring before she could draw a drop of water, and then she had to carry her full pails all the way to the top again.

But all the same 'twas a good spot for a house in one way, for being perched up like that at the very top of Knockmany Hill, Fin could see all ways—North, South, East and West—and that gave him a good warning if any of his enemies should take it into their heads to pay him a visit. Fin wasn't one to like being taken by surprise. He had yet another way of getting a warning, as well as keeping a good look-out. He would put his thumb into his mouth till it touched one special tooth, right at the back, and then the thumb would tell him what was coming to pass.

Well, one day, when all seemed peaceful, Fin was sitting with his wife, Oonagh, when she saw that he had put his thumb in his mouth.

'What are you doing that for, Fin?' says she.

'Oh, my grief and sorrow, he's coming!' said Fin as soon as he had pulled out his thumb and could speak plain, and she saw that he looked as miserable as a wet Sunday.

'Who's coming?' asked Oonagh.

'That horrid beast of an old Cucullin, no less,' answered Fin.

Now, as Oonagh well knew, though Fin was near as tall and big as a round-tower, Cucullin was bigger still and was an enemy that Fin didn't want to meet, no not for all the world. All the giants for miles around were afraid of Cucullin. When he was angry and gave a stamp with his foot, the whole country shook. Once, by a blow of his fist, he had flattened a thunderbolt till it was flat as a pancake, and ever after he kept it in his pocket to show to anyone who offered to fight with him. Fin was a match for most of the rest of the giants, and had even boasted that the great Cucullin had never—so far—

come near him for fear he would get a drubbing. But now, oh grief and sorrow! Cucullin, no less, was on his way, and Fin didn't like the idea—no, not at all!

'How to get round such a terrible fellow, or what to do, I don't know,' went on Fin to his wife in a very doleful tone. 'If I run away while there's still time I shall be a laughing-stock to all the other giants, and a terrible disgrace will be on me. But how to fight with a giant that makes a pancake out of a thunderbolt with one blow of his fist, and that shakes the whole country with one stamp of his foot, I don't know!'

'How far has he got?' asks Oonagh.

'As far as Dungannon,' answers Fin.

'How soon will he be here?' asks she.

'Tomorrow about two o'clock,' answers he, and then he adds with a groan, 'And meet him I shall for my thumb tells me so.'

'Now, now, my dear! Don't fret and don't be cast down!' answers Oonagh. 'Let's see if I can't be the one to bring you out of your great trouble!'

'For the love of all the saints, Oonagh my darling, do what you can! Else for sure I'll either be skinned like a rabbit before your eyes, or else have my name disgraced before the whole tribe of giants. Oh, my grief! Oh, my sorrow! If this isn't just a regular earthquake of a fellow, and him with a pancake in his pocket that was once a thunderbolt!'

'For shame on you, Fin! Be easy now! Pancake, did you say? See now if I can't treat that bully boy to some feeding that'll give him a sore tooth! Leave your moaning and lamenting now, Fin! If I can't get round and circumvent that great lump of a fellow, never trust Oonagh again.'

With that she went to where her skeins of wool were hung out to dry after she had dyed them and she took nine long strands of all the colours she had. She platted the wool-threads three and three, and when it was done she tied one plait round her right arm, one round her right ankle and the third and longest she tied right round her, over her heart.

She'd done all this several times before, when Fin was in trouble, so his mind got a bit firmer when he saw what she was at, for the truth is she hadn't ever failed yet when she had got the threads on her.

'Is there time for me to go round to the neighbours?' Oonagh asked.

'There is time,' said Fin. So off she set and she went to this one and that. When she came back Fin saw that she had borrowed a whole load of griddles—which are thin irons, like huge plates, for making scones or flat bread over a turf fire. Then he saw how she kneaded enough dough to make as many griddle loaves as she had irons. One she cooked in the proper way and made a good round flat loaf of it—big as a cart-wheel nearly—but all the rest were made in a very strange way, for she made them two-sided, each with an iron griddle hidden in the middle. As each one was done, she put it away in the bread-cupboard. Then she made a big milk cheese and she boiled a whole side of bacon, set it to cool, and began to boil a sackful of cabbages.

By this time it was evening, the evening of the day before Cucullin was to come, and the last thing Oonagh did was to light a high smoking bonfire on the hill outside and to put her fingers in her mouth to give three whistles. This was to let Cucullin know that strangers were invited to Knockmany, for that was the way that the Irish, long ago, would be giving a sign to travellers that they could come in. Oonagh didn't tell Fin about her plans that night, but she did ask him a few things about Cucullin, and one of the things that Fin told her was that Cucullin's mighty strength lay in just the one place, and that was the middle finger of his right hand.

Next morning, as you can guess, Fin was on the lookout, and after a while he saw how his enemy Cucullin—as tall as a church tower—was striding along across the valley.

Back into the house went Fin and his face was as white as Oonagh's milk cheese when he was telling her the news. But Oonagh only smiled, she had something ready for Fin too.

'Now Fin dear! Take it more easy! Be guided by me. Here's the cradle that the children are too old for now,

and here's a white bonnet, and here's a nightgown of mine that will look for all the world like a baby's robe when you have it on over your shirt. Dress yourself up, lie down snug in the cradle, and cover yourself with the quilt, say nothing, and be guided by me, for this day you must pass for your own child.'

Fin was shaking with fear and he was scarcely tucked up, when there came a regular thunder of a knock on the door.

'Come in and welcome!' cried Oonagh, and, with that, a great huge man twice as big as old Fin, opened the door. And who was it but the mighty Cucullin himself, as punctual to his time as the stars themselves.

'God save all here,' says he in a great rumbling voice. 'And is this where the famous Fin lives?'

'Indeed and it is! Come in and rest, honest man.'

'It's Mrs. Fin you'll be?' says he, coming in and sitting down.

'Indeed and I am, and a fine strong husband I have,' says she.

'Aye,' says he, 'he has the name of being one of the best giants in Ireland, but all the same there's one come that is very willing to try to get the better of him in a fair fight.'

'Dear me!' says Oonagh. 'Isn't that a grievous pity now, for he left the house in a fury this very morning at the first of the light. Word had come that a great big bully of a giant by the name of Cucullin had gone down to look for him on the northern coast of the sea—the place where the Irish giants are building their causeway to get to Scotland. Saints above! But I hope for the poor ignorant fellow's sake that he doesn't find Fin, for Fin'll make paste of Cucullin this day, he's in such a fury!'

'It's I am Cucullin, and it's I that am after fighting with Fin!' answered Cucullin, frowning. 'This twelvemonth I'm after looking for him, and its Fin that will be ground to paste, not me!'

'My sorrow! I'm thinking that you never saw Fin,' said Oonagh, shaking her head.

'How could I see Fin,' answered Cucullin, 'and him dodging all the while to get away from me like as if he was a snipe on a bog?'

'Fin dodging to get away from you, is it, you poor little creature?' says Oonagh. 'I tell you it'll be the black day for you if ever you do see Fin, and let's only hope the wild furious temper that is on him now will have cooled a bit, or else it's rushing to your death you'd be. Rest here a while and when you go it's me that will pray to the holy saints that you never catch up with Fin.'

Cucullin began to wonder a bit about such words, so he didn't speak for a while, and presently Oonagh said, looking about her:

'Isn't that just a terrible wind that's blowing in at the door and making the smoke come down! Fin always helps me when it does that. As he's from home, perhaps you'd be civil enough to do the job for me?'

'What job is that?' asked Cucullin.

'Oh, just to turn the house round for me. That's what Fin always does.'

This made Cucullin wonder a bit more. However, he got up and then Oonagh noticed that, as he stood there,

he pulled at the middle finger of his right hand till it gave three little cracks, and she remembered how Fin had told her that it was in this finger that Cucullin's mighty strength lay.

Well, after that he stumped outside on his great legs, put his two great arms round the house and turned it round, just as Oonagh had asked him to do.

Fin, hiding in the cradle, felt ready to die with fear to see the like of that, for of course he never *had* turned the house for Oonagh, no, not in all the long time they'd been married.

But Oonagh, who was outside with Cucullin, gave a sweet smile and a plain 'thank you' making out that turning a whole house round was as easy as opening a door.

'Since you're so civil, perhaps you'd do another obliging thing for me, Fin being away,' says she.

'What obliging thing is that?' asked Cucullin.

'Nothing very great,' says she. 'But after this spell of dry weather, we've been after enduring, I'm having to go down the hill for every drop of water. Only last night Fin promised me he'd get at a spring of water there is under the rocks at the back. But he left home in such a temper, chasing after you to fight you, that he forgot all about it. I'll have a bite of dinner ready for you, if you'll just pull the rocks asunder for me.'

So she brought Cucullin down to see the place, and indeed it was all rock and part of the mountain itself, with only one small crack in it, so that you could scarcely hear the water gurgling underneath.

It was plain from the look on Cucullin's face that he didn't like the job. However, he pulled his finger three times and took another look, then he pulled it three times again, and had another look, and still he didn't like what he saw, for the job was no less than to rend the mountain itself.

However, after he had pulled his finger yet three times more—that was nine times in all—he stepped down. This time he tore a great cleft in the side of the mountain, and it was four hundred feet deep and half a mile long. (It's there to this day—Lumford's Glen they call it.)

'That's very obliging of you I'm sure,' says Oonagh. 'And now away back to the house, for you to get a bite of dinner, for Fin would be blaming me if I let you go without, even if you are enemies, and even if it's only our own humble fare that I can set before you.'

Fin, you remember, was still in the cradle, and hadn't seen what had been going on outside, but all the same he was quaking and shivering to see Cucullin coming back with Oonagh and sitting down at the table.

Oonagh served the giant with two big cans of butter, the whole side of bacon, and she had the whole sack of cabbages ready boiled for him. Last of all she brought out a pile of the big round flat loaves that she had baked the day before.

'Help yourself, and welcome,' says she.

So Cucullin started on the bacon and cabbages and then he picked up one of the big flat loaves and opened his mouth wide to take a huge bite out of it. But he had scarcely bitten into that bread before he let out a terrible yell.

'Blood and fury!' cries he.

'What's the matter?' asks Oonagh.

'Matter enough!' cries he. 'Here's two of my best teeth cracked. What kind of bread is this?'

'Why,' said Oonagh, making out that she was very much surprised, 'that's only Fin's bread! Even his child in the cradle there can eat it!' With that she took the one flat loaf that hadn't got a griddle inside it, and she went across to Fin where he lay in the cradle, and gave him the bread and a hard nudge.

Cucullin watched, and sure enough the thing in the cradle took a huge bite out of the bread and then started munching.

'Here's another loaf for you, Cucullin!' says Oonagh, shaking her head as if she pitied him. 'Maybe this one'll be softer for you.'

But this one had a griddle inside it as well, and when he tried to bite it Cucullin let out a yell that was louder than the first, for he'd bitten harder, not liking the way Oonagh had seemed to pity him.

This yell of Cucullin's was so loud that it frightened Fin into letting out a yell as well.

'There now, you've gone and upset the child!' says Oonagh. 'If you're not able to eat Fin's bread, why can't you say so quietly?'

But Cucullin hadn't got an answer to that, for he was beginning to feel a bit frightened. What with turning the house, and what with tearing up the mountain, and now what with seeing Fin's child, though it was still in its cradle, munching that terrible bread before his very eyes, he was beginning to think that it really was a good thing he hadn't found Fin at home. Maybe all that Oonagh had been telling him was nothing but the truth!

'And is it special teeth they all have in Fin's family?' asked Cucullin at last, nursing his own jaw. His mouth was too sore for any more bacon and cabbage.

'Would you like to feel for yourself?' answered Oonagh 'I'll get the little fellow to open his mouth for you. But perhaps you'd be afraid of him? It's rather far back in his mouth his teeth are—just put in your longest finger!'

Well, can you guess now what happened? Indeed perhaps you'd hardly believe it, if you didn't know already that there's hardly an end to the foolishness of giants. Yes, that was it!

Cucullin, with a little bit of help from Oonagh, was so foolish as to put in that one special finger of his, the middle finger of his right hand, right into Fin's mouth! Well, maybe Fin wasn't the bravest or the wisest, but all the same he was wise enough to give a good hard bite when he had such a chance as that! So now there stood Cucullin without his finger, and worse than that, without his strength. So at last, Fin plucked up his courage, jumped out of the cradle and then Cucullin thought best to run for it.

Away and away, all down Knockmany Hill Fin chased him, for if Cucullin's strength was gone, he could still run. So at last, since he couldn't catch him, Fin came back, and by then Oonagh had taken the griddles out of the loaves. So the two of them sat down in peace to eat what was left of the dinner that clever Oonagh had set for Cucullin.

THE WELL OF THE WORLD'S END

Long ago there lived a girl who had a stepmother. One day the stepmother gave her a sieve and told her to go and fill it with water from the Well of the World's End.

'Mind you bring it home to me full,' says the stepmother.

At that the girl was very sad, for she didn't know how to find the place, and as for filling a sieve with water that was a second thing she didn't know about. However, off she started, with a heavy heart. As she went she asked everyone she met where the Well of the World's End might be. But nobody knew, and she couldn't tell what to do. At last she met a queer old woman, all bent double.

'Can you tell me, please,' says the girl, 'where to find the Well of the World's End?'

The old woman answered her kindly and told her just where it was, and how she was to go. So the girl thanked her, did just as the old woman said, and, sure enough, she did find the well.

But dear, dear, her troubles weren't ended yet, for, as you can guess, each time the girl dipped the sieve into the cold, cold well, the water all ran out of it again. The

girl tried and she tried, but it was no use, so at last she sat her down on the edge of the well and she cried as if her heart would break.

Suddenly she heard a strange croaking voice.

'What's the matter, my dear?' said the voice, and with that she looked up. There sat a huge frog with large round eyes looking at her.

'What's the matter, my dear?' said the voice again, and then she saw that it was the frog that was speaking.

'Matter enough!' said the girl, still crying, and then she told the frog how hard it had been to find the well and what her stepmother had said, and how, every time she dipped the sieve in the well, all the water ran out.

'If you promise,' said the frog, 'to do whatever I tell you for a whole night long, I'll help you.'

'How?' asked the girl.

'I'll tell you how to fill your sieve with the water,' answered he.

The frog seemed friendly enough.

'And what harm can a frog do me anyhow?' thinks she. So she promised.

Then said the frog in its strange croaking voice:

'Stuff it with moss and daub it with clay
And then it will carry the water away.'

No sooner had it said the last word than it gave a jump and Plop! Splash! It disappeared into the cold dark water of the Well of the World's End.

The girl did just as the frog had told her; she found some moss and she stuffed it into the holes in the sieve. Then she found some clay and she daubed on the clay very carefully. Then she let it all dry a bit in the sun, and at last, once more, she dipped the sieve into the cold, cold water of the well. This time the water didn't run out and, with a light heart, the girl started off home. As she went she turned to have a last look at the Well of the World's End and, as she looked, the frog popped his head out of the water again and called out:

'Remember your promise!'

'All right,' says she, and she thought again, 'What harm can a frog do to me?'

So back she went and, this time, the way didn't seem long at all and she brought the sieve full of water to her stepmother.

That very evening, as the two of them sat by the fire, they heard something tapping at the door, low down. Then a voice said:

'Open the door, my honey, my heart,
Open the door, my own darling;
Mind you the words that you and I spoke,
Down at the World's End Well.'

Now of course the woman was surprised to hear that, but the girl knew well enough what was at the door, and so she told her stepmother all about it.

'Girls must keep their promises,' said the woman. 'Go and open the door.'

So the girl got up, and she opened the door. Sure enough, there was the great frog on the doorstep, and it was so wet that the water ran off the step and down the path. The frog gave a hop, right into the room and when the girl took a step back to go to her chair it took another big hop after her. Then it looked at up her with its great round eyes and it said:

'Lift me to your knee, my honey, my heart,
Lift me to your knee, my own darling;
Remember the words that you and I spoke,
Down by the World's End Well.'

Well, the girl did not much like the idea of that, for the frog was dripping wet. But the woman said again:

'Girls must keep their promises.'

At that down the girl sat close to the fire again, and she lifted the frog on to her lap, and it was so wet that her apron and her dress were soon both soaked through and the frog was so cold that it seemed to the girl as if the fire gave no heat. For a long while they sat like that and the frog said never a word. At last it spoke again:

'Give me some supper, my honey, my heart,
Give me some supper, my darling;
Remember the words that you and I spoke,
Down by the World's End Well.'

The girl was glad enough to do that, so she got up and sat the frog on the chair, but the frog was so wet that the water ran down to the floor. The girl made ready a bowl of bread and milk, and she fed the frog with a spoon, and when it had finished it said:

'Take me to your bed, my honey, my heart,
Go with me to bed, my own darling;
Mind you the words you spoke to me,
Down by the cold well so weary.'

Well, the girl did not want to do that! She didn't want to take the cold wet thing into her bed, but the woman said again:

'Girls must keep their promises!'

So sadly and sorrowfully the girl took the frog with her to bed and, as you can guess, she kept it as far away from her as she could. It's little sleep she got that night.

Just as dawn was beginning to break, she heard that the frog was speaking again. This time it said:

'Chop off my head, my honey, my heart,
Chop off my head, my own darling;
Remember the promise you made to me,
Down by the cold well so weary.'

Now the girl was sorry to hear the frog say that. She didn't want to harm it. She remembered how it had been kind to her, and how it had taught her how to fill the sieve with water and, wet and cold though it was, she began to think it was quite a pretty sort of creature. So for a while she didn't do anything. Soon the frog said again in its queer croaking voice:

'Chop off my head, my honey, my heart,
Chop off my head, my own darling;
Remember the promise you made to me,
Down by the cold well so weary.'

When the girl still didn't want to do it, the frog repeated the words yet a third time. So then she saw there was no help for it. She went and she found the axe, and she put the frog on the floor, then, with tears running from her eyes, she chopped off its head.

Then what do you think happened? There in front of her, instead of the frog, stood a handsome young Prince. He didn't speak with a frog's croaking voice any more, but with his own clear voice, and he took the girl by the hand and he told her how he had been enchanted by a wicked witch and that the girl had broken the spell for him. The spell had been that, in his frog state, he had to find a girl who would do his bidding for a whole night.

So they were married and they went to live in the castle of the King his father, and there was great rejoicing, because now, at last, the spell was off, and he was a Prince again.

THE GOOD OLD MAN

Long ago, in Wales, a good old man and his good old wife lived in a little white cottage not far from Snowdon. Every evening, after supper, before they sat down by the fire, the old man would take the bucket with all the greasy water, in which his wife had done the day's washing-up, and he would walk just ten steps from the door of the little white cottage till he got to the garden wall. Then he would empty the bucket over the wall, carefully swishing out all the greasy water and onion-skins and potato-peelings and carrot-scrapings and whatever else there might be. Next morning the neighbour's pig would come rooting and snuffing for whatever hadn't soaked into the ground. The old man liked to see that.

Yes, indeed! He was a nice kind old man that one, and his wife was very glad that he did this for her every evening while she tidied up the hearth and made the fire bright.

One evening, just when the moon was rising, the old man went out as usual. Ten steps he walked from the door of his little white cottage. He was just going to pour the bucket out over the garden wall as usual, when he noticed that somebody was standing by the wall beside him. It was a stranger, someone that he had never seen before. He was a funny little fellow was this stranger. He was dressed in green with a red waistcoat, and his clothes were made in a way the old man hadn't seen, no, not for years. He had queer squinty eyes, and beside all that the old man noticed that he had very big feet.

'Oh dear! Oh dear!' said the stranger, the squinty-eyed fellow. 'Indeed I do wish you wouldn't do that every evening!' and he pointed to the bucket. The good old man was surprised.

'Well, really now! I've done it every evening of my life!'

'Yes, indeed! I know you have!' said the squinty-eyed stranger and he gave such a deep sigh that the good old man felt quite sorry.

'But what harm can it do?' asked the old man.

'Harm enough!' said the squinty-eyed stranger.

'But the neighbour's pig, now! He likes it very much, for he comes every morning snuffling for the potato-peelings and the onion-skins and the carrot-peelings, and whatever else there may be,' said the old man.

'I know very well that he does,' said the queer stranger, and he sighed again, and then he added, 'Do you think you could stand on my feet?'

'Stand on your feet?' said the good old man. 'What help would that be?'

'It would be a great help, because then I could show you what is the matter,' said the stranger and, this time, he seemed more down-hearted than ever.

'Well, I could try,' said the old man, for he was always one to be kind. So the stranger came up close beside the man, who had a good look at him.

'Dear me!' thought the good old man. 'What a good thing it is that the squinty-eyed fellow has got those big feet! For they really are big enough for me to be able to stand on them'—when he was holding on to the wall as well, you understand.

As he stood on the queer stranger's feet, and as he held on to the wall, the good old man looked down to where he'd always poured out the bucket, and what do you think! It seemed as if he could look right down into the ground, just as if it had been clear water, and there, just below, what should he see but a cottage, a white cottage that was very much like his own. But oh dear! What a mess! The slates on the roof were all running with grease and pig-swill! There were potato-peelings tangled round the chimney, and onion-skins in the gutter, and the water-butt was all nasty with carrot-scrapings and whatever else there was.

'Dear me,' said the old man as he looked, 'who would have thought it!'

'It comes right down my chimney,' said the stranger and he sounded very down-hearted, just as if he were going to cry, 'right down my chimney it comes! Some-

times it splashes into the room, and even when it comes outside, it splashes on the window-panes. And my wife is so down-hearted, she's ready to die, for how can she keep a clean house with pig-swill running down it for thirty years?'

'Man dear! But it's terrible!' said the good old man, still looking down. 'But I don't know how I can help it—not really. Every night I come out of my house and I walk ten steps from the door, and what would my poor wife say if I didn't empty the bucket for her? Getting old, she is!'

'Could you think of a way to stop it?' said the stranger, sighing.

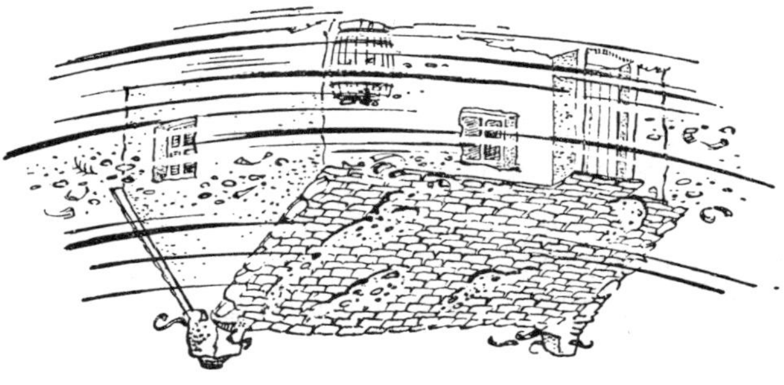

'Yes, I could think! But truth to tell I don't know what to think!' said the good old man at last, and with that he got off the queer stranger's feet and then he couldn't see anything any more—except what he'd always seen, and except the queer stranger himself. Then the two of them sat down, and now the good old man felt very sad indeed, thinking of all the pig-swill on the nice tidy house.

There they sat for a long time. 'We haven't thought of anything,' said the squinty-eyed fellow at last. 'So I will come back in three days' time, and perhaps by then you will have thought.' And with that they both sighed and said good night.

When he got back to the cottage the good old woman was wondering what had kept her old husband out in the moonlight so long. Then he told her all about it.

'Dear me!' she said, and now she too was ready to cry. 'What a terrible thing indeed for that poor woman to have all that pig-swill pouring over her roof and down her chimney every night!' And after that they went to bed, both feeling very down-hearted.

Next morning when it was daylight, they both leaned over the wall, but they couldn't see anything except the pig snuffling about, very well pleased, as usual, and the ground looked exactly as it had always looked. So they went back to the little white cottage. For three days they sat, and they talked and talked about what they could do, and each evening the good old man emptied his pig-bucket as usual, but he sighed as he did it.

On the third night the old man went out, wondering if the queer stranger would come as he had said. It was dark, for the moon hadn't risen yet, but all the same it was light enough for him to see that the queer stranger really was there again, and so they greeted each other.

'My heart has been sore for you indeed with the pig-swill running down your chimney,' said the good old man. 'And my wife has been fit to cry only with the telling of it.'

'Have you thought of anything?' asked the stranger sadly.

'Well, indeed I have!' said the good old man.

'And does the good old woman agree with it?' asked the stranger.

'Yes indeed, she does,' said the good old man.

'And what is it?' asked the stranger.

'It's this,' said the good old man. 'To move the door of my house and make an opening on the other side, and to pay Mr. Williams, joiner, and Mr. Bill Davies, mason, to do a tidy job for me—for indeed I'm too old now to do it myself! But I and my wife, we can't bear to think that you and your good woman should live like that with the pig-swill all over a nice tidy house for thirty years! No indeed! Really.'

And that is just what the good old man did, and that is why—to this day—that little white cottage has the door on the wrong side of it. He paid Mr. Williams, joiner, and Mr. Bill Davies, mason, for the work they did—that good old man. But do you know, all the same, it didn't cost him a penny? For what do you think? Every Saturday night, after it was dark, the good old man or the good old woman would always find an old-fashioned silver penny pushed under their new door.

THE HAIRY BOGGART

Long ago, in Lincolnshire, it used to be all dykes and ditches between the fields and the farms. At Numby, there lived a farmer named Mr. Nasche, and, since he was doing well, he thought he'd take over a new bit of land that joined his own fields. Very cheap he got it too. Indeed he couldn't help wondering why he didn't have to pay more; still he was very well pleased.

Well, after he'd ridden into the town and got the buying all settled up with the lawyers, towards evening he went along to look at his new field. He walked along slowly, thinking where he could put a new gate and also a bit of a bridge across the dyke. For he would need one for getting his cart and his ploughs and that across.

But no sooner had he jumped over the dyke on to his new ground, than what should he see coming towards him but a great hairy Boggart! A great big thing it was, and it had arms almost as long as the shafts of a cart.

'What ar't doing walking about over my land?' says Boggart, very surly.

'*Your* land?' says Mr. Nasche and would have liked

to say a lot more, only he didn't dare to treat that Boggart anything except nice and civil, for it looked as strong as a six-year old horse.

'My land it be!' growled Boggart.

Well they set to and argued about it. Mr Nasche said it was his land, and wouldn't give in, but Boggart wouldn't give in neither, so, as they couldn't agree which had a right to the land, the farmer said they'd better go to law about it.

'Nay!' says Boggart. 'I'll have naught to do with law, that's never done me justice!' So it seemed there would be no end to the argument. But at last Boggart suggested that they should share the crops equally, but that the farmer was to do the work. Mr. Nasche thought about that, but really he didn't see why he should do all the work and yet share with that nasty hairy old Boggart. However he thought what he'd do.

'Very well,' says Mr. Nasche at last. 'Us'll share! But which will you have—what grows above ground, or what grows beneath ground? Only mind! You'll have to stick to what you settles; I don't want no back-reckoning after!'

Well, Boggart thought a bit, and then he said he'd have what grew above ground for his share, and so it was settled, and Mr. Nasche said once more that there was to be no complaints. But what did Billy Nasche do? He ploughed and then he planted that whole field with potatoes!

So you see, when harvest time came, and the Boggart came along for his share, he didn't get a single potato—only the withered old tops! Nothing at all but the haulms and the twitch!

That Boggart was so angry you wouldn't believe! He

shook his great fist at the farmer, but of course Mr. Nasche and he had agreed right from the start that there wasn't to be any back reckoning. Boggart had agreed to that months ago.

Well, Boggart swore he wasn't going to be taken in like that again, so he said that, next season, he was going to have all that grew below ground.

Billy Nasche made haste to agree to that, and once more he ploughed up the ground, and when it was all ploughed, what did he do but sow wheat!

So, when harvest time come round again, the Boggart was more furious than ever, for he had to stand there and see Billy Nasche getting in a lovely crop of corn and straw, and nothing was left for Boggart but the worthless roots and stubble.

Boggart was as mad as a bull!

'You false, cunning, weasel of an old web-footed yellow-bellied cheating fen-man you!' bellowed he to the farmer, shaking his great hairy fist and fairly dancing

with rage. 'Next year you'll sow wheat again! But this time you and me'll reap together! You'll start this end of the field, and I shall start t'other, and each'll take what he reaps.'

You see, Boggart reckoned that, since he was as strong as a six-year-old horse, he'd have reaped the whole field before Mr. Nasche had fairly started.

Well, Billy Nasche he didn't know what to say to that! But Boggart looked so mad and furious that at last he had to agree. So when the time came, he ploughed, and then he sowed the wheat. He was in a puzzlement, but scratch his head as he would, for a long time he couldn't see a way to get the better of the Boggart. After a bit the wheat began coming along nicely, and every Sunday, when Mr. Nasche went to look at it, it went more and more to his heart to think that that beautiful crop of corn was mostly growing for that nasty, lazy, hairy old Boggart.

Now there was a Wise Man that lived nearby. They

say he was born on St. Mark's Eve—seventh son of a seventh son they say he was; anyhow, he was a Wise Man and able to tell the future.

One evening, without telling anyone where he was going, Mr. Nasche went to him and asked him what he should do about that beautiful field of wheat. And when the Wise Man had made a bit of a spell, he told him something that made the farmer go away very well pleased and thinking that the pay he had to give the Wise Man was money well spent.

Next day (though it wasn't Sunday) Nasche went to look how the wheat was growing, and he thought to himself that it wouldn't grow any taller now—only ripen. Then after he'd had this good look, what should he do but go to the blacksmith, and he asked the blacksmith would he please make him a lot of thin iron rods just as long as that wheat was high.

Next day—or maybe it was the day after—the rods were ready, and when he'd got them, he stuck them all about among the standing wheat—but only at the Boggart's end of the field.

So when the wheat stood heavy-headed and golden, and when a fine and lovely day for reaping was come, Mr. Nasche and the Boggart they both started, one at one side of the field and one at the other. Each of them was looking very well pleased too, because, you see, each was thinking how they were going to do the other one!

Well, Mr. Nasche was a good reaper and he got along fine, but as for the old Boggart he didn't know what it was that was wrong, for he wasn't very bright and he never noticed that he was trying to reap iron rods as well as corn! He couldn't get along at all! He had to stop to whet his reaping-hook (because the rods were taking all the edge off it); and he had to keep stopping to rest (because the iron rods were wearing down his strength)! And all the while Mr. Nasche he went along swinging steady as anything and piling up the sheaves into stooks. And so they worked all that fine and lovely day, and the sun blazed over them.

At last Boggart was so vexed he let out a screech and he flung down his reaping-hook.

'You may take the mucky old land!' Boggart screamed out. 'The mucky old land and all that's on it. I won't hev no more to do wi' it!'

Off he went in a screaming temper! Off he went and he never came back! Anyhow not into Mr. Nasche's field. After that he just mooned about the dykes and the ditches, and if you leave your dinner or your tools about, it's often that very same Boggart that makes off with them.

THE FALSE KNIGHT

'Oh, where are ye going?' quoth the false knight upon the road.
'I'm going to the scule,' quoth the wee boy, and still he stood.
'What is that upon your back?' quoth the false knight upon the road.
'Ah weel, it is my books,' quoth the wee boy, and still he stood.
'What's that you've got in your arm?' quoth the false knight upon the road.
'Ah, weel, it is my peat,'[1] quoth the wee boy, and still he stood.
'Wha's aucht all they sheep?' quoth the false knight upon the road.
'They are mine and my mither's,' quoth the wee boy, and still he stood.
'How many o' them are mine?' quoth the false knight upon the road.
'A' they that have blue tails,' quoth the wee boy, and still he stood.
'I wish ye were on yon tree,' quoth the false knight upon the road.
'And a good ladder under me,' quoth the wee boy, and still he stood.
'And the ladder for to break,' quoth the false knight upon the road.
'And you for to fall down,' quoth the wee boy, and still he stood.
'I wish ye were in yon sea,' quoth the false knight upon the road.
'And a good bottom[2] under me,' quoth the wee boy, and still he stood.
'And the bottom for to break,' quoth the false knight upon the road.
'And ye to be drowned,' quoth the wee boy, and still he stood.

[1] The boy's bit of peat is his contribution to the school fire [2] Ship or boat

THE BLACK BULL OF NORROWAY

Once upon a time—up in the north they say it was in one of those parts where England joins Scotland—there lived a lady and she had three daughters. The oldest of them said to her mother:

'Mother, bake me a bannock, and roast me a collop, for I'm going away to seek my fortune.'

Her mother did this, and the daughter went away to an old witch washer-wife and told her what she wanted. The old wife bade her stay a while, and look out of the back door each day, and see what she could see. She saw nought the first day. The second day she looked, and saw nought. On the third day she looked again, and saw a coach-and-six coming along the road. She ran in and told the old wife.

'Yon's for you,' said the old woman. So they took the girl up into the coach, and galloped off.

Later on the second daughter says to her mother:

'Mother, bake me a bannock, and roast me a collop, for I'm going away to seek my fortune.'

Her mother did this, and away she too went to the old witch washer-wife. On the third day, when she looked out of the back door, she saw a coach-and-four coming along the road.

'Yon's for you,' said the old woman. So they took her up, and off they set.

At last the third daughter wanted to go off, just as her sisters had done, and she too went to the witch washer-wife, who, once again, told the damsel to look out of her back door every day and see what she could see. She did so; and the first day when she came back she said she had seen nought. The second day she looked and saw nought. The third day she looked again, and then she came back and she said to the old wife that she saw only a great Black Bull coming crooning along the road.

'Yon's for you,' said the old witch. The young damsel was next to distracted with grief and terror, but, for all that, she was lifted up and set on his back, and away they went.

Far they travelled, and far they travelled, till the damsel grew faint with hunger.

'Eat out of my right ear,' says the Black Bull, 'and drink out of my left ear, and set by what you can't eat.'

So she did as he said, and was wonderfully refreshed. And long they rode, and hard they rode, till they came in sight of a fine great castle.

'Yonder we must be this night, for my oldest brother lives there,' said the Bull, and presently they were at the place. They lifted her off his back, and took her in, and him they sent away to a field for the night. In the morning they took the lady into a fine shining parlour, and gave her a beautiful apple, telling her not to break it till she was in the greatest strait ever mortal was in in the world, and that would bring her out of it. Again she was lifted on the Bull's back, and after she had ridden far, and farther than I can tell, they came in sight of an even bonnier castle, and far farther away than the last. Says the Bull to her:

'Yonder we must be this night, for my second brother lives there,' and they were at the place directly. They lifted her down and took her in, and sent the Bull to the field for the night. In the morning they took the lady into a fine and rich room, and gave her the most beautiful pear she had ever seen, bidding her not to break it till she was in the greatest strait ever mortal could be in, and that would get her out of it. Again she was lifted and set on the bull's back, and away they went. And long they rode, and hard they rode, till they came in sight of the biggest castle, and the farthest off, that they had seen yet.

'We must be yonder tonight,' says the Bull, 'for my youngest brother lives there,' and they were there at once. They lifted her down, took her in, and sent the Bull to the field for the night. In the morning they took her into a room, the finest of all, and gave her a plum, telling her not to break it till she was in the greatest strait mortal could be in, and that would get her out of it. Then they brought home the Bull, set the lady on his back, and away they went.

And on they rode, and on they rode, till they came to a dark and ugsome glen, where they stopped, and the lady lighted down off the Bull's back. Says the Bull to her:

'Here you must stay till I go and fight the Old 'Un. You must seat yourself on that stone, and move neither hand nor foot till I come back, else I'll never find you again. And if everything round about you turns blue, that will mean that I have beaten the Old 'Un; but should all things turn red, he'll have conquered me.' So the damsel set herself down on the stone, and by and by all around her turned blue. Overcome with joy, she lifted one of her feet, and crossed it over the other, so glad was she that her companion was victorious. But though the Bull came back and sought long for her, he could not find her.

Long she sat, and long she wept, till she wearied. At last she rose and went away, she didn't know where. On she wandered, till she came to a great hill of glass. She tried all she could to climb it, but wasn't able. Round the bottom of the hill she went, sobbing and seeking a way over, till at last she came to a smith's house; and the smith promised, if she would serve him for seven years, then he would make her iron shoes, and then she would be able to climb over the glassy hill.

At seven years' end she got her iron shoes, and she climbed the glassy hill, and where should she find she had got, but to a place where lived another old witch washer-wife.

There she was told of a gallant young knight that had given in some clothes to wash that were all over blood, and whoever washed them clean was to be his wife. The old wife had washed till she was tired, and then she had set her daughter at it. They had washed and they had washed, in hopes of getting the young knight, but for all they could do, they couldn't bring out even one stain. So now, at length, they set the strange damsel to work, and as soon as she began, all the stains came out pure and clean, but the old witch washer-wife made the knight believe it was her daughter had washed the clothes. So the knight and the witch's daughter were to be married, and the stranger damsel was distracted at the thought of it, for she loved the knight. So she bethought her of her apple, and breaking it, she found it filled with gold and precious jewellery, the richest she had ever seen.

'All these,' she said to the witch's daughter, 'I will give you, on condition that you put off your marriage for one day, and allow me to go into the knight's room alone at night.'

So the false bride consented, but meantime the old witch-wife had prepared a sleeping-drink, and given it to the knight, who drank it, and so he never wakened till next morning. But all the live-long night the damsel sobbed and sang:

‘Seven long years I served for thee,
The glassy hill I clomb for thee,
Thy bloody clothes I wrang for thee;
And wilt thou not waken and turn to me?’

Next day she knew not what to do for grief. Then she broke the pear, and found it filled with jewellery far richer than had been in the apple. With these jewels she bargained for leave to be a second night in the young knight's chamber; but the old witch-wife gave him another sleeping-drink, and he again slept till morning. All night the damsel kept sighing and singing as before:

‘Seven long years I served for thee,
The glassy hill I clomb for thee,
Thy bloody clothes I wrang for thee;
And wilt thou not waken and turn to me?’

Still he slept, and she nearly lost hope altogether. But next day, when he was out hunting, one of the hunting party asked him what the noise and moaning was that had been heard all last night in his bedchamber. He said:

'I heard no noise.'

But they told him again that there had been strange sounds of weeping and he resolved to keep watch that night.

That being the third night, and the damsel being between hope and despair, she broke her plum, and it held far the richest jewellery of the three. She bargained as before, and the old witch-wife, as before, took in the sleeping-drink to the young knight's chamber, but he told her he couldn't drink it that night without sweetening. So she went away to fetch some honey to sweeten it with, and then he poured out the drink, but he made the old wife think he had drunk it. The knight went to bed again, and the damsel began her watch and, as before, she began singing:

'Seven long years I served for thee,
The glassy hill I clomb for thee,
Thy bloody clothes I wrang for thee;
And wilt thou not waken and turn to me?'

This time the knight heard, and he turned to her, and she told him all that had befallen her, and he told her how he had been enchanted into the form of a bull but, having defeated the Old 'Un he had been given back his human shape. He had looked long for her in the magic glen.

So next day the old washer-wife and her daughter were chased away and the knight and the damsel were married and for aught I know, he and she are living happy to this day.

MR. AND MRS. VINEGAR

There were once two people who lived in a vinegar bottle with a wooden door. Their names were Mr. and Mrs. Vinegar.

Now Mrs. Vinegar was a clean sort of a body and one day she was busy sweeping her vinegar-bottle house when, by ill luck, what should happen but that the end of her broom-handle should hit the wall—*thump!* Down came the whole house in bits, clitter-clatter, and Mrs. Vinegar was nearly buried in broken glass.

Out she rushed to find Mr. Vinegar.

'Oh, Mr. Vinegar,' cried she, 'such a dreadful thing has happened! We're quite ruined! I've knocked the wall with the end of my broom and now the whole house is all smashed into little pieces!'

Mr. Vinegar tried to comfort his wife as well as he could.

'We shall have to do the best we can, my dear. Perhaps we had better go out into the world to seek our fortune. See,' said he when he had had a look, 'the door is still all right. I'll take it along with us on my back. It's sure to come in useful.'

So off they went, trudging along. When night came they were both very tired, and by then they had got to a thick forest.

'My love,' said Mr. Vinegar, 'I'll tell you what we'll do. I'll climb up into that tree over there, pull up the door after me, and then wedge it safe on that strong branch. You shall climb up after me, and then we shall be able to sleep quite safely.'

So this was done, and the two of them stretched themselves carefully out on the door and went to sleep.

In the middle of the night they were woken up by the sound of voices under their tree.

'Here's five pounds for you, Jack,' said a deep bass voice, and then there was a clink of money and another voice said, 'Thank 'ee, Captain!'

Then the name of Bill was called out, and Bill was given three pounds. It seemed as if Bill wasn't best pleased with this. Then, as the voices went on, some one called Bob got ten pounds as his share.

Mr. and Mrs. Vinegar began to feel more and more

afraid that the men under the tree could be nothing more or less than a gang of robbers who were busy dividing up the money that they had stolen.

Now Mr. and Mrs. Vinegar had always been most respectable and this idea frightened them so much that they both began to shake and tremble and, as the door hadn't been very firmly wedged, the end of it was that though the pair of them managed to cling to the branches of the tree, the door fell thump, right on to the heads of the robbers.

Now, of course, it was the robbers' turn to be afraid. Away they scampered in terror, but neither Mr. nor Mrs. Vinegar knew for certain that they had gone, so they didn't dare to come down out of the tree till daylight.

Then, at last, Mr. Vinegar did scramble down, lifted up the door, and there, on the ground, what should he find but all the golden guineas that the frightened robbers had left behind them.

'Come down, Mrs. Vinegar,' he called out in delight. 'Come down! Our fortune's made!'

Mrs. Vinegar came down as fast as ever she could. My! How pleased she was by the sight of all that money. They began to count it and found to their delight that they had got forty guineas.

'My dear,' says Mrs. Vinegar, 'I'll tell you what we'll

do. You take all this money to the fair and buy a cow. I know how to make splendid butter and cheese, and then, for ever after, we shall be able to make a fine living.'

Now that very morning was the morning of the fair, so Mr. Vinegar agreed, took the money, and off he went to buy a cow.

He hadn't been long at the fair before he saw a beautiful red cow that was for sale. She seemed to be an excellent milker too.

'Oh, what a beautiful cow,' said Mr. Vinegar to himself, 'if only I had her I should be the happiest man alive!' So he offered to pay his whole forty guineas for the cow. Now cows were sold much cheaper in those days than they are now and though she was a good cow and a good milker, it wasn't at all wise of Mr. Vinegar to pay all that money for her. However, of course the man who was selling the cow didn't think it was *his* business to tell Mr. Vinegar that he was paying too much. So, what he did was to praise the cow a great deal and then pretend that he was letting her go cheap because he liked Mr. Vinegar.

So silly Mr. Vinegar paid over all the money and then began to lead the cow out of the sale-ring.

Now all round about, the rest of the fair was going on,

with stalls and music and so on, and as Mr. Vinegar and his cow went along, he saw a man who was playing the bagpipes. This man was making a fine noise with his tunes. All the children were following him round, and the people were clinking money into his cap whenever he held it out. Mr. Vinegar listened and looked, and thought it was wonderful.

'Oh,' said Mr. Vinegar to himself, 'what a splendid way of making a living! If only I had those bagpipes I should be the happiest man alive!' So after a while he went up to the man and said:

'Those are wonderful bagpipes you've got there! What a lot of money you seem to be getting, and all just for playing on them!'

'Yes,' said the man, 'they really are wonderful bagpipes and I do make a lot of money. It's a fine life!' Well, the end of it was, that the man, never dreaming that Mr. Vinegar would be so silly as to agree, offered to exchange the bagpipes for Mr. Vinegar's beautiful red cow.

'Done!' said Mr. Vinegar, delighted.

But, as you can guess, Mr. Vinegar hadn't any idea of how to play a proper tune on his new bagpipes. He puffed and he blew, and he squeezed and he squeezed, but all he could get out of those bagpipes was a most doleful, direful, moaning, screeching and groaning. So, of course, instead of crowding round and giving him money, all the grown-up people hurried off as fast as ever they could and some of the children even began to throw mud at him.

So there was nothing for it, but for him to go away. Now as he went, the day began to cloud over and to grow chilly, and poor Mr. Vinegar began to feel cold. Just as he began to think how cold he was, he met a man who was wearing a pair of nice thick gloves.

'Oh,' said Mr. Vinegar out loud, 'how cold my hands are! If I only had a pair of nice thick gloves I should be the happiest man alive!'

The stranger heard what he said and answered:

'Yes, it has turned cold. And yet with these gloves my hands are as warm as could be.'

'I wish I had a pair of gloves like yours,' said Mr. Vinegar.

Well, the end of it was that the man offered to let him have the gloves, if he got the bagpipes in exchange.

'Done!' said Mr. Vinegar. He gave the man the bagpipes and put on the warm gloves.

Then for a while he felt perfectly happy, and he went on his way back to Mrs. Vinegar.

But it was quite a long walk, so at last Mr. Vinegar began to feel tired, and just as his legs began to ache he saw a man who was walking along, with a good stout stick.

'That's a good stick you've got,' said Mr. Vinegar. 'If only I had that stick I should be the happiest man alive!'

'Yes,' said the man, 'it's a good stick and it's been a good friend to me for many a long mile. But I don't mind letting you have it in exchange for that pair of warm gloves you are wearing.'

'Done!' said Mr. Vinegar, delighted, and taking off the gloves, away he went with the stick.

And now as he walked and got nearer to where he had left Mrs. Vinegar, he began to look at the stick, and then to look at the hedges, and he noticed that, in the hedges, there grew sticks which were just as good as the one he had got in his hand. After that he began to think over all the bargains he'd made that day, and how he had started out with forty golden guineas, and how he had ended up with a stick. He could see now, that it was no better than one he could have cut for nothing, out of the hedge.

Just as he was thinking all this, he saw a jay flying among the trees, and next moment the jay began to call:

'Ha ha! Ha ha!' for all the world to hear, and if you ever heard a jay calling you'll know that it sounded exactly as if the jay was laughing at Mr. Vinegar.

'You impudent bird!' he called out in a fury. 'How dare you laugh at me!' and with that he threw his stick at the bird which only flew away Ha ha-ing and laughing more than ever. But as for the stick, it lodged in the branches of one of the trees and though Mr. Vinegar tried to climb the tree and get it, and though he tried to shake it down, it was all in vain.

So the end of it was that Mr. Vinegar got back to Mrs. Vinegar with nothing at all to show for the forty guineas, and he sat down beside her on the ground, and they just looked at each other and for all I know they are both sitting there to this day.

But some say that, after that, they grew wiser, and found another vinegar-bottle that someone had thrown away, and so, in this way, they managed to set up their house again.

THE BAKER'S DAUGHTER

Why does the owl cry 'Woo-hoo' so miserably all night long? If you want to know, it fell out like this.

In the old, old times—not in your time nor yet in mine—there were, as you know, many Strange Beings about in England. There were The Little People and Laidly Worms, Giants, Speaking Toads, and so on. Also there were fairies that were very great and powerful. These fairies would often go about disguised as mortals and they used to find out about many secret deeds and who did good and who did evil.

One evening, one of these powerful fairies disguised herself as a poor old beggar-woman. Hobbling in her tatters through a certain village in Herefordshire, she went into the bakery. The shop was rather dark inside, and smelt of new bread and, at the back, glowed the great, hot baking-oven. At the front of the shop a pretty, trim girl—the baker's daughter—was working briskly. She had fresh, crisp loaves piled up on a big trestle-table, and she had the dough set to rise in a crock near the fire, and more dough in a big kneading-trough. The fairy saw how, when it was time, the girl would take a batch of finished loaves out of the glowing oven, and put in a new lot of risen dough that she had ready. When she had got a batch out she tapped each warm loaf with her knuckles to hear if it was rightly baked and then she put it with the others on the trestle-table.

'Spare a bit of bread for a poor old woman!' said the beggar in a feeble voice.

The baker's daughter was stooping to the oven, and just glanced up at the poor old thing as if she were not worth looking at, and then, crossing over to the covered crock, but with never a good wish or a civil word, she pulled off a small bit of risen dough and gave it to her.

'I haven't got a bit of fire in my cottage,' said the old woman, holding the dough in her trembling hand. 'Give me leave to put this in the oven with the rest of the batch.'

Well, the baker's daughter was almost too proud to look at the old woman. However, she let her put the little piece of dough on to the long wooden shovel that she used for putting in the loaves, and when it was time for the next batch to go in she pushed the bit of dough into the oven to bake with the rest. But then, when she took out the batch of loaves she saw that something strange had happened—the beggar's small bit of dough had swelled so much that it was the biggest loaf of the lot. The old woman put out her hand for it, but the baker's daughter snatched it away.

'Get away, you dirty old woman!' said she. 'That's not your loaf!'

Plead as the old woman would, the baker's daughter wouldn't let her have it. Indeed, it was as much as she would do to give the fairy another piece of dough, and the bit she gave her now was even smaller than the first.

Once more the same thing happened; the little piece of dough swelled in the oven till it was bigger than the first one had been, and once more the proud baker's daughter refused to give it to her and tried to drive the old woman away. Only after much pleading did she give the old beggar a third piece—and this was the smallest of all.

Now, as I have told you, the baker's daughter was so proud that she would scarcely glance at the old woman. If she had taken the trouble to look, she would have noticed something. For when the third scrap of dough came out of the oven as a loaf that was bigger than either of the first two, and when for the third time the girl wouldn't give away such a handsome loaf, a change had come over the old beggar. She was bent no longer, but very tall. Now her rags were rags no more, but she was dressed in a shining mantle, while the crooked stick on which she had leaned had become a straight, gleaming wand.

At last, however, the baker's daughter did look up, and when she saw she trembled and sank to her knees, and she offered to give all the bread in the shop to the fairy. But it was too late.

'So it's you who have been cheating all the poor people of the village!' said the fairy in a stern voice. It was no good for the baker's daughter to say that indeed, indeed it wasn't she. The fairy raised her wand and struck the baker's daughter one blow. Immediately the proud girl shrank and changed, and in another moment she flew out of the window in the shape of a brown owl.

And to this day you may hear her, when evening comes, flying round the churchyard, or else flitting from one elm tree to another, crying and lamenting:

'Too-whit-too-whoo! My feet are cold!'

THE KING OF THE CATS

There was once, in a certain parish in England, a man whose job it was to ring the church bell for the services, to look after the churchyard, and dig the grave when anyone had to be buried.

He lived with his wife near the church, and they had a very fine cat—coal-black he was, with one white spot on his chest, and his name was Old Tom.

One winter's evening when the man had been out most of the day digging a grave, his wife and Old Tom sat by the fire waiting to have their tea till he should come back. They waited, and they waited, and still he didn't come, but at last, in he rushed, calling out:

'Who's Tom Tildrum?' and he looked so wild that both his wife and the cat fairly stared at him.

'What's the matter?' asked his wife.

'I've just heard and seen such queer things, you'd hardly believe!' said the man.

'Sit down quick then, and tell us about it,' said his wife.

Well, the man was in a great hurry to tell and though

the kettle was boiling he sat down at once, opposite his wife, with Old Tom on the hearth-rug between them.

'I was busy digging a grave,' says he, 'for that old fellow that's to be buried tomorrow, and I'd gone down pretty well as deep as need be, it was getting dusk and I was standing down in the grave, shovelling out the last spadefuls when I heard a something calling out "Miaou".'

'Miaou,' said Old Tom, as if in answer.

'Yes! Just like that,' said the man nodding. 'So I looked up and what do you think I saw?'

'How can I tell?' answered his wife.

'Well, it was nine black cats, each one with a white spot on his chest, just like our Old Tom, and what do you think they were doing? They were carrying a little small coffin. It was covered with a black velvet pall and on the lid was a little small gold crown. They were coming along very slowly, and at every third step they all called out, "Miaou!".'

'Miaou!' said Old Tom again.

'Yes! Just like that,' said the man. 'Well, they were coming nearer and it seemed as if they were going to pass quite close, and I could see that eight of them were carrying the coffin, and that the ninth—the biggest one—was walking in front for all the world like . . . But wife! Just look at our Old Tom! You'd think he was listening to every word!'

'Never mind Old Tom,' said his wife. 'Go on.'

'Well, there they were, coming nearer and nearer, and at every third step crying "Miaou" . . .'

'Miaou!' cried out Old Tom again.

'Yes, just like that,' said the man, 'and just as they were going past the grave where I stood watching them, they all stopped and they all looked straight at me . . . But wife! Just look at Old Tom! He's looking at me just as they did!'

'Go on, for pity's sake!' cried his wife. 'Never mind Old Tom.'

'Well then, the one that was walking in front—the one that *wasn't* carrying the coffin it was—came up close, and it said to me—yes, I tell you, it *said* to me, in a squeaky voice, "Tell Tom Tildrum that Tim Toldrum's dead!" But, oh dear wife! How can I tell Tom Tildrum that Tim Toldrum's dead, if I don't know who Tom Tildrum is?'

'Look at Old Tom!' called out his wife. 'Just look at Old Tom!'

And well they might look! For Old Tom was standing

up, and his fur was stiff up on his back, and he was looking twice the size, and his tail was like a big black bottle-brush, and his great green eyes were staring at them. And then, as they watched him, what did he do but call out in a squeaky voice:

'If Tim Toldrum is dead, then I'm the King of the Cats!' And with that, up the chimney he sprang and they never saw him again.

THE CAULD LAD OF HILTON

At a big house called Hilton Hall, there once lived a Brownie.

Now you must know that such Brownies are rather like lobs or pisgies. That is, they're mostly nice but contrary creatures, that'll sometimes help and sometimes hinder with the work of a farm or house. There was one Brownie they tell about in Cornwall that would work all night long at threshing corn and do more in the time than a man could have done, but he would only work if they remembered to set a good bowl of Cornish cream for him. Then there was another—a famous one, who was called 'Robin Goodfellow'. He was as bold as a bullfinch and would play all kinds of tricks, such as spilling the ale just as some old lady was going to drink, or letting all the farm horses out of the stable and then leading them into a bog. He always laughed and laughed at his own jokes.

Now the Hilton Hall Brownie wasn't as bad as Robin Goodfellow, nor as good as the one in Cornwall. Sometimes he was as helpful as could be, and sometimes he was up to all kinds of mischief. If he was in a bad mood, he would go round the house after the servants had gone to bed, and would put the sugar into the salt-cellars and the salt into the beer, he would rake out the fires that had been carefully banked up for the night, and he would empty away the pails of fresh water that had been drawn from the well ready for the morning.

And yet, if he was in a good mood, there was no end to the help he would give. When they got up in the morning the servant-girls would find that half the work had been done for them, They would find the rooms cleaned, the hearths swept, bright fires, a tidy kitchen, and any sooty pots and pans, and any dull, scratched pewter mugs and plates, all shining and burnished, and that the kitchen table and the chopping-block had been scrubbed white. This was generally if they'd remembered to set a bowl of cream for him, or else a good slice of bread and honey.

Now one night the servants happened to sit up late, they'd been telling old tales round the fire, laughing and singing. Two of the girls—the dairy-maid and the scullery-maid—were creeping quietly upstairs to bed, so

as not to wake the older servants, or the gentry, when one of them thought she heard a noise in the kitchen. Now no one had ever managed to catch sight of the Brownie, so the girls crept down the stairs again and made bold to open the kitchen door a crack, in hopes of seeing him.

Sure enough, there he was, and what do you think he was doing? He was swinging himself to and fro—sitting in the hook of the long chain that they used for hanging the pots on down over the fire. As he swung, he was singing in a very doleful voice:

'Woe's me! woe's me!
The acorn's not yet
Fallen from the tree,
That's to grow the wood,
That's to make the cradle,
That's to rock the child,
That's to grow to the man,
That's to lay me.
Woe's me! woe's me!'

Now these were kind-hearted girls, and as they were getting undressed that night, they began talking in whispers, and they both agreed that it was a shame for the poor Brownie to be there against his will, for, after all, he looked a nice little thing, and if he had often done them a mischief, he had just as often done them a good turn. So they agreed together that, next chance they had, they would try to find out how he could be set free to go off wherever he wanted.

So next day they began asking this one and that how he was to be freed, but no one could tell them anything. At last they asked the henwife.

'Good gracious!' said she. 'It's easy enough to send a

Brownie on its way,' and then she told the girls what they must do.

Now the Fair was on at the nearest town and the girls asked leave to go, and they each took a part of their wages and, with the money, they bought some cloth of Lincoln green. They knew they wouldn't need very much for, as they had seen, this Brownie was only a small little creature. All next evening they cut and they sewed, and out of the green cloth they made a neat little cloak with a hood to it. When it was ready they laid it by the kitchen hearth; then, creeping away, they waited and watched through a crack.

They hadn't waited long, when sure enough, they saw the Brownie. He had a frown on his face too and was looking as if this was one of the evenings when he was bent on mischief.

But when he spied the little green cloak, oh what a change! He began to smile and grin. He held up the cloak to see it better, then putting it on, he admired himself in a well-polished copper pan, and then started to frisk and dance all round the kitchen. As he danced, he sang these words, over and over again:

'I've taken your cloak, I've taken your hood,
The Cauld Lad of Hilton will do no more good.'

Then, still frisking and dancing for joy, he vanished, and was never seen or heard of again.

A SPADEFUL OF EARTH

There was once a wicked old giant that lived just across the Welsh border, and why it was I don't know, but certain it is, that he hated the Mayor and all the people of Shrewsbury.

He thought, and he thought of what he could do to spite them all. At last, what did the wicked old thing hit upon, but to take a great spadeful of earth and lam it down just where it would dam up the River Severn.

'That'll make the river overflow,' thought he, 'and that'll drown the whole town—Mayor, and people, and all.'

Well, he set off, the spiteful creature, with the biggest spadeful of dirt that even such a huge fellow as he could carry. Now, how it came about I also don't know, but anyhow certain it is that he missed his way and after a while it wasn't Shrewsbury at all he got to, but near to Wellington. By that time it was evening, and the weight of that huge great spadeful of dirt was making him fairly puff and blow, and hope he was near the end of his journey.

By and by, as he went, the giant met a cobbler carrying a sack of old boots and shoes on his back. This cobbler was on his way back to Wellington where he had his shop, and the boots and shoes belonged to his Shrewsbury customers and were all for mending.

'I say!' called out the giant. 'How far is it to Shrewsbury?'

'Shrewsbury?' asked the cobbler, looking up, and looking up, till at last he could see the top of that great giant, and then, not liking the looks of him at all, 'And what may you be wanting at Shrewsbury?' said he.

'D'you see this big spadeful of dirt?' said the giant in his great rumbling voice. 'I'm a-going to lam all this into the River Severn, and fill it up so's to make a flood to drown Shrewsbury—Mayor, and people, and all.'

Now the cobbler didn't like the idea of that.

'Drown Shrewsbury?' thought he, 'Mayor, and people, and all? That'll never do!' But how was a little fellow like him to stop a great fellow like the giant? That was a fair puzzle. The cobbler put down his sack and he scratched his head, and at last he said:

'Shrewsbury is it? That's a long, long way. You'll never get to Shrewsbury tonight, nor yet tomorrow.'

'How do you make that out?' said the giant.

'Look at me, I've just come from Shrewsbury,' says the cobbler, opening his sack, so's the giant could see what was in it. 'It's such a long way, I've had time to wear out all these boots and shoes on the road.'

Well, now it was the giant's turn to be in a puzzle.

'Oh, deary me!' said he, with a great groan, and a sigh like a gale of wind. 'Then it's no use! For I'm fairly tired out already! Carry this great spadeful of dirt any farther I can't and I won't.'

'Well it's a terrible long way,' agreed the cobbler, hoping that, in the dusk, the giant wouldn't catch sight of Shrewsbury itself, for it lay quite close at hand.

'Perhaps the best would be for me just to drop my spadeful here, and go home,' said the giant. And again the cobbler said nothing but hoped the giant wouldn't catch sight of what he didn't want him to see.

But the giant was that vexed that he saw nothing. He just lammed down that great lump of earth exactly where he stood, and then he scraped his boots on the spade, and off he trudged back to Wales, and nobody in Shropshire ever saw or heard anything about him again.

And to prove that this tale is true, everyone who goes to Shrewsbury can see the great Wrekin hill standing there to this day. Even the dirt that the wicked old thing scraped off his boots can be seen. It's the little Ercall hill standing close by the Wrekin's side.

CAP O' RUSHES

There was once a very rich gentleman, and he had three daughters.

One day he thought he would like to see how fond they each were of him. So he says to the first:

'How much do you love me, my dear?'

'Why,' says she, 'I love you as I love my life.'

'That's good,' says he. So he says to the second, 'How much do you love me, dear daughter?'

'Why,' says she, 'I love you better than all the world.'

'That's good,' says he. So he says to the third, 'How much do *you* love me, my dear?'

Now the youngest daughter didn't like this sort of a question, and she didn't believe that her sisters really loved their father as much as she did. She tried to laugh it off, so she said:

'I love you as much as fresh meat needs salt.'

Well, the old gentleman didn't think that a question like that was anything to laugh about, so he fell into a passion.

'That means you don't love me at all, you ungrateful thing,' says he, 'in my house you shall stay no more.'

The end of it was that nothing she could say would persuade him of the truth which was, that she did love him the best, and he shut his door on her so that all she had got to go out into the wide world with were three dresses.

However, there was nothing for it, away she had to go. On and on she went, till she came to a watery, squelchy bog. And there she gathered a lot of rushes, and she plaited them up till she made a kind of a cloak with a hood to it, and when she put it on, the cloak covered her from head to foot. After that she went up on to higher ground and hid her three fine dresses under the dry roots of a tree. Then on she went again till at last she came to a great house.

'Do you want a maid?' says she.

'No, we don't,' says they.

'I haven't got anywhere to go.' says she, 'and I'd ask no wages, and do any sort of work.'

'Well,' says they, 'if you like to wash the pots and scrape the saucepans, you can stay.'

So she stayed, and she washed the pots and scraped the saucepans, and did all the dirty work. And because she didn't tell them any name, they called her Cap o' Rushes.

One day there was to be a great dance a little way off, and the servants where she worked were allowed to go and look at the grand people. But Cap o' Rushes said she was too tired to go, so she stayed at home.

But when all the others were gone, she offed with her cap o' rushes and she washed herself in the clear water of the brook, and she went back to the fen and put on a silver dress and went to the ball. And of all the fine folk who were dancing there, there was none so fair or so finely dressed as she.

Who should be at the ball, but her master's son, and what should he do but fall in love with her the minute he set eyes on her. He wouldn't dance with anyone else.

But before the dance was done, Cap o' Rushes slipped off and away she went home. When the other maids got back she was pretending to be asleep with her cap o' rushes on.

Next morning, they said to her:

'You did miss a sight, Cap o' Rushes!'

'What was that?' says she.

'Why, the beautifullest lady you ever did see, dressed right gay and gallant. The young master he never took his eyes off her.'

'Well, I should have liked to have seen her,' says Cap o' Rushes.

'There's to be another dance this evening, and perhaps she'll be there.'

But, come the evening, Cap o' Rushes again said she was too tired to go with them. However, when they were gone, she offed with her cap o' rushes, washed herself in the brook, went back to the fen, and this time the dress she put on was one made all of gold.

The master's son had been reckoning on seeing her, and again he danced with no one else, and never took his eyes off her.

But before the dance was over she slipped off. Home she went, and, when the maids came back she pretended to be asleep with her cap o' rushes on.

Next day they say to her again:

'Well, Cap o' Rushes, you should'a been there to see the lady. There she was again—right gay an' gallant. As for the young master, he never took his eyes off her.'

'Deary me,' says she, 'I should have liked to have seen her!'

'Well,' says they, 'there's a dance again this evening, and you must go with us, for she's sure to be there.'

Well, come the evening, Cap o' Rushes said for the third time that she was too tired to go, and do what the other servants would to persuade her, she said she would stay at home. But when they were all gone, she offed with her cap o' rushes, and bathed herself in the brook, went back to the fen, and this time she put on a dress that was made of the feathers of all the birds that fly in the air. And then, once more, away she went to the dance.

The master's son was rarely glad when he saw her. He danced with none but her, and never took his eyes off her. But she wouldn't tell him her name, nor where she came from, but at last he gave her a ring, and told her if he didn't see her again he should die.

The dance wasn't over when off she slipped away just as before. Home she went, and when the maids

came back she was pretending to be asleep with her cap o' rushes on.

Next day, they said to her:

'There, Cap o' Rushes! You didn't come last night, and now you won't see the lady, for there's to be no more dances.'

'Well, I should have rarely liked to have seen her,' says she.

The master's son tried every way to find out where the lady was gone, but go where he might, and ask whom he might, he never heard a thing about her. And he got worse and worse, and at last he had to keep his bed he was so ill for the love of her.

'Make some gruel for the young master,' they said to the cook, 'he's very sick and near dying for love of the lady.'

The cook had only just set about making the gruel when Cap o' Rushes came in.

'What are you doing?' asks she.

'I'm going to make some gruel for the young master,' says the cook, 'for it seems that he's near dying for love of the lady.'

'Let me make it,' says Cap o' Rushes.

Well, the cook wouldn't at first, but at last she agreed; and so it was Cap o' Rushes that made the gruel. When she had made it, she slipped the ring into it on the sly, before the cook took it upstairs.

The young man he drank it, and then he saw the ring at the bottom.

'Send for the cook,' says he. So up she comes again.

'Who made this gruel?' says he.

'I did,' said the cook, for she was frightened, you see, but he just looked at her.

'No, you didn't,' says he. 'Say who did, and you shan't be harmed.'

'Well, then, 'twas Cap o' Rushes,' says she.

'Send Cap o' Rushes here,' says he. So Cap o' Rushes came up.

'Did you make the gruel?' says he.

'Yes, I did,' says she.

'Where did you get this ring?' says he.

'From him that gave it me,' says she.

'Who are you, then?' says the young man.

'I'll show you,' says she. And she offed with her cap o' rushes, and there she was in her beautiful clothes, and her long lovely hair hung to her waist.

The master's son he got well very soon, and they were to be married in a little time. It was to be a very grand wedding, and everyone was asked from far and near. Cap o' Rushes' father was one of those that was asked. But nobody knew that he was the bride's father, for still she wouldn't tell anybody who she was.

But before the wedding she went to the cook.

'I want you to dress every dish of meat without putting a mite o' salt in it,' says she.

'That'll be rare and nasty,' says the cook.

'Never you mind for that,' says she.

Well, the wedding-day came, and they were married. And after they were married, all the grand company sat down to the wedding feast.

But when they began on the meat, it was so tasteless, they couldn't eat it. Cap o' Rushes' father, he tried first one dish and then another, and then, what did he do but burst out crying.

'What's the matter?' said the master's son to him.

'Oh,' says he, 'I had a daughter, and I asked her how much she loved me! And she said, "As much as fresh meat needs salt". And I turned her away from my door, for I thought she meant that she didn't love me. But now I see that she meant that she loved me best of all. And she may be dead now for aught I know.'

'No, father, here she is!' says Cap o' Rushes.

And with that she started up from her place and she ran to him and put her arms round his neck.

And so they all lived happy ever after.

HARDY HARDBACK

One time there was an old King, very rich he was, and he had a witch, and he was very proud of all the magic that this witch could do. But there was one thing she couldn't do, and that was to break the spell that was on the King's daughter—the youngest one.

So this King sent out a proclamation to say that if there was anyone in the kingdom who could, first, do more than his old witch could, and could break the spell as well, then he should have his youngest daughter and half the kingdom; but if they tried and couldn't, then they would have their heads cut off.

Now there were three brothers, Will, Tom and Jack. Sons of poor people they were, who lived in a little cottage, and when they heard what the king had said in the proclamation, they all three decided that they'd try.

So first Will told his mother that he was going to the King's house to see if he could break the enchantment of the lady. Since he had a long way to walk, his mother cooked him some food to take with him.

Well, Will started out, and by and by he met a little dried-up old man. This little old man said:

'Good morning, Will.'

Will said:

'Good morning.'

'Where are you going to?' said the little dried-up man.

'That's none of your business,' says Will.

So Will went on and he tramped all the long way to the King's house, and he hollers out:

'Hallo!'

The King came out and said:

'What'll you have?'

'I came over,' Will says, 'to see if I can break the enchantment of the lady.'

The King says:

'Well, remember; if you can't do as much as my old witch can do, I'll have to cut your head off.'

'I know that,' says Will.

King says:

'Do you think you can hit the iron hackle as hard as my witch can?' (Hackles you know, are made of iron spikes. They used them in those days to tease out wool and flax).

'Yes, bedad, I think I can.'

'Come, old witch,' King says, and she put her back against that hackle, and popped like a rubber ball and danced all over the floor. Will came in and he too put his back against that hackle, but he pushed so hard he pushed the spikes right through him and it killed him.

So then Tom said he wanted to go. His mother said:

'Oh, Tom, don't go, Will got killed.'

'Well, bedad, I'm going anyway,' says Tom.

So she cooks him up some food and Tom, he starts out, and he meets the same little old dried-up man that

Will met, and the very same thing happened, for he wouldn't tell the little dried-up old man where he was going. The King told him he'd got to hit the iron hackle with his back as hard as the old witch did, or else, if he liked, he could find someone that could do it for him. Well, Tom said he'd try himself. But the very same thing happened that happened to Will.

Next Jack decided he wanted to go, and he got to begging his mother to cook him up a bag of food. Mother said:

'Now Jack, don't go! You're all we've got.'

Jack said he was going anyway. But his mother burst out crying and she wouldn't cook up any food, so he just took some old dried bread and started out. By and by Jack met the same little dried-up man.

'Good morning, Jack,' Man says.

'Good morning, Father,' Jack says, 'Good morning, Uncle, have some breakfast with me.'

'Where are you going to, Jack?'

'Well, Uncle, I'm going to try to make a ship that'll sail on dry land.'

'You take my stick, Jack, and you go back the way I've come till you get to a spring. You stir my stick in that there spring until the spring turns to wine, and you'll see a new tin bucket and tin cup as well. By the time you get back here I'll have your ship made.'

So Jack went and, sure enough, he found the spring

and he stirred it until it turned to wine, and there sat the bucket and the tin cup. He filled the bucket and came back, and the little old man had the ship made, and they sat down and ate their bread and drank their wine. The old man said:

'Jack, you get into this ship and say, "Sail, ship, sail", and it'll sail, and you take into the ship every man that you see between here and the King's house. Whenever you see a man you say, "Hey! What's your name?" and when he tells you you must say, "Come here and get in this ship", and you'll say, "Sail, ship, sail", and it'll sail right along.'

So Jack got into the ship and said:

'Sail, ship, sail,' and it did. As he was sailing along, and looking up at the mountains, he saw a man hitting his back against the trees and so strong he was knocking them every which way. Jack says:

'Hey! What's your name?'

'Hardy Hardback.'

'Hardy Hardback? Hardy hard back I think you are! Come and get in here.'

So the man got in with Jack.

They sailed on a little way, and he saw a man out in the pasture just eating up the sheep and hogs.

'Hey! What's your name?' calls out Jack.

'Eat Well.'

'Eat Well? Eat well I think you are! Come and get in here.'

So the man got into the ship along with Jack and the other one. They sailed on a little way and Jack saw a man down in a hollow just drinking up all the little springs and brooks.

'What's your name?' calls out Jack.

'Drink Well.'

'Drink Well? Drink well I think you are! Get in here.'

So Drink Well got in along with Jack and the other two, and Jack said:

'Sail, ship, sail,' and it sailed right on.

They sailed for a while and then Jack saw a man running. He'd run for a bit of a way on one leg, and then run a while on t'other. Jack says:

'Hey! What's your name?'

'Run Well.'

'Run Well? Run well I think you are! Come, get in here.'

So Run Well got in too and they sailed right on, till they came to a man standing with a gun, and it looked just like he was shooting a hare in the skies.

'Hey! What's your name?' calls out Jack.

'Shoot Well.'

'Shoot Well? Shoot well I think you are!' says Jack. 'Come on, get in here.'

So he got in with Jack and the other four, and Jack said:

'Sail, ship, sail,' and they sailed right on. They sailed till they came to a man a-listening. He'd put one hand behind one ear, and one behind t'other.

'Hey! What's your name?' says Jack.

'Hark Well.'

'Hark Well? Hark well I think you are! Come on, get in here.'

So Hark Well got in with Jack and the other five and Jack says:

'Sail, ship, sail,' and it sailed right on.

At last they got to the King's house and Jack hollered out:

'Hallo!'

Then the King came out and said:

'What'll you have?'

Jack says:

'I came over to see if I could break the enchantment of the lady.'

'Well, remember, if none of you can do as much as my old witch can, I'll have to kill you.'

'Yes, I know it,' says Jack.

'Do you think you could hit the iron hackle as hard as my old witch can, or can you find anyone else that can?' says the King.

'Yes, bedad, I think I can.'

So the King called his old witch, and she stabbed her back against the iron hackle and bounced off like a rubber ball, and danced all over the room.

'Hardy Hardback, come in here,' says Jack. Hardy

Hardback came in and he hit that iron hackle with his back and stove it through the wall, and then he jumped and danced all over the place.

'Well, now, do you think you can eat as much as my old witch can, or can you find anyone that can?' asked the King.

'Yes, I think so. Come in here, Eat Well!' So Eat Well came in and they gave him and the old witch a horse each. Eat Well ate up his horse, and a cow or two, and a couple of sheep, and some pigs, and the old witch didn't get even one horse eaten up. Said the King:

'Well, now do you think you can drink as much as my old witch can, or can you find anyone who can?'

'Yes, I think so,' says Jack. 'Drink Well, come in here.' So they showed them each a stream, and Drink Well drank his up and a spring or two, and was drinking the river up when they called in the King.

'Well now,' says the King, 'can you find a man that can run as fast as my old witch can?'

'Yes, I think so. Run Well, come in here.'

So they gave 'em an eggshell each and started them off to run to the ocean to fetch back an eggshell full of salt water. Run Well got on to the ocean first, and he got his water and came on back and met the old witch still going with an empty eggshell and only half-way to the ocean. Said she:

'I'm tired.'

'I'm tired too,' said he.

'Let's sit down and rest,' says she, 'and not run ourselves to death for other people.'

So they went up above the road a few steps to a nice grassy place, and sat down.

'Lay your head over here and rest,' says she.

Now the old witch had an old jaw-bone in her pocket, and if she could get anybody to sleep and put that under their head, they wouldn't wake up until that old jaw-bone was knocked out. So she waited till Run Well was asleep, and she put that jaw-bone under his head. She poured the salt water out of his eggshell, and started on to the ocean.

Jack began to get uneasy and said:

'Hark Well, hark well and see where Run Well's got to.'

'Jack, I tell you he's laying asleep half-way between here and the ocean, with an old jaw-bone under his head, and he'll never wake till that's knocked out.'

'Shoot Well, shoot well and shoot it out,' says Jack.

So Shoot Well shot and knocked the old jaw-bone right out from under his head. Then Run Well jumped up and picked up his eggshell and started to the ocean. When he was coming back he caught up to the old witch and he knocked her over and came on back to the King's house.

The end of it was that Jack and the Princess were married before the old witch got there, and when I left, they was rich.

THE STRANGE VISITOR

A woman was sitting at her wheel one night;
And still she sat, and still she span, and still she wished for company.

In came a pair of broad broad soles, and sat down at the fireside;
And still she sat, and still she span, and still she wished for company.

In came a pair of small small legs, and sat down on the broad broad soles;
And still she sat, and still she span, and still she wished for company.

In came a pair of thick thick knees, and sat down on the small small legs;
And still she sat, and still she span, and still she wished for company.

In came a pair of thin thin thighs, and sat down on the thick thick knees;
And still she sat, and still she span, and still she wished for company.

In came a pair of huge huge hips, and sat down on the thin thin thighs;
And still she sat, and still she span, and still she wished for company.

In came a wee wee waist, and sat down on the huge huge hips;
And still she sat, and still she span, and still she wished for company.

In came a pair of broad broad shoulders, and sat down on the wee wee waist;
And still she sat, and still she span, and still she wished for company.

In came a pair of small small arms, and sat down on the broad broad shoulders;
And still she sat, and still she span, and still she wished for company.

In came a pair of huge huge hands, and sat down on the small small arms;
And still she sat, and still she span, and still she wished for company.

In came a small small neck, and sat down on the broad broad shoulders;
And still she sat, and still she span, and still she wished for company.

In came a huge huge head, and sat down on the small small neck.

'How did you get such broad broad feet?' quoth the woman.

'Much tramping, much tramping!' (*gruffly*).

'How did you get such small small legs?'
'Aih-h-h!—late—and wee-e-e-moul!' (*whiningly*).

'How did you get such thick thick knees?'
'Much praying, much praying!' (*piously*).

'How did you get such thin thin thighs?'
'Aih-h-h!—late—and wee-e-e-moul!' (*whiningly*).

'How did you get such big big hips?'
'Much sitting, much sitting!' (*gruffly*).

'How did you get such a wee wee waist?'
'Aih-h-h!—late—and wee-e-e-moul!' (*whiningly*).

'How did you get such broad broad shoulders?'
'With carrying broom, with carrying broom!' (*gruffly*).

'How did you get such small small arms?'
'Aih-h-h!—late—and wee-e-e-moul!' (*whiningly*).

'How did you get such huge huge hands?'
'Threshing with an iron flail, threshing with an iron flail!' (*gruffly*).

'How did you get such a small small neck?'
'Aih-h-h!—late—and wee-e-e-moul!' (*pitifully*).

'How did you get such a huge huge head?'
'Much knowledge, much knowledge!' (*keenly*).

'What did you come for?'
'FOR YOU!'

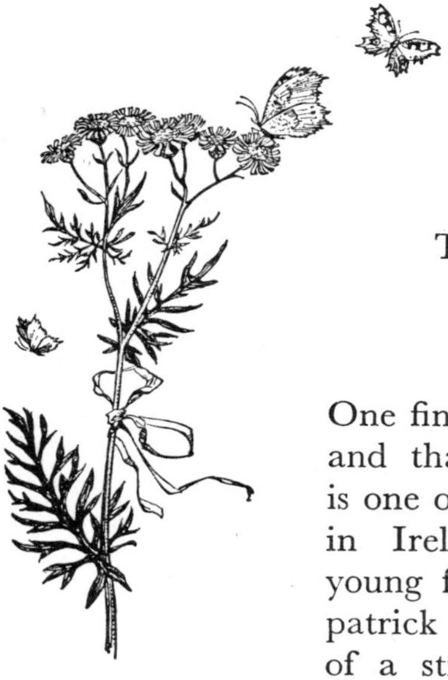

THE FIELD OF BOLIAUNS

One fine day—Lady-day, it was, and that, as everybody knows, is one of the greatest of holidays in Ireland—one fine day, a young fellow named Tom Fitzpatrick was taking an easy sort of a stroll in the fields, going slowly along the sunny side of a hedge. All of a sudden, he heard, low down, a small click-clacking sort of a noise in the hedge.

'Isn't it surprising now,' said Tom to himself, 'to hear the stonechatters singing at this season?'

So Young Tom stole on, going on the tips of his toes now to try if he couldn't get a sight of the bird—just wanting, you understand, to know if he was right in his guess. Then, as he looked sharply through the bushes, he saw something. It wasn't a bird that he saw, but a great big brown pitcher, that might hold about a gallon and a half; and stranger still, close by it, sat a little wee teeny tiny bit of an old man. He had a little cocked hat stuck upon the top of his head, and a deeshy daushy sort of a leather apron and, as Tom watched, the little fellow pulled out a little wooden stool, stood up upon it, dipped a little piggin jug into the big pitcher, took out the full of it, and put it down beside the stool. Then he sat down again close under the pitcher, and began to work at putting a heel-piece on a little bit of a brown brogue shoe just fit for himself, and the knocking of it was this very same small click-clack of a sound that Tom had first heard.

'Well, by the powers!' said Tom to himself, 'I often heard tell of the Lepracauns, but Truth! I never rightly believed in them—but here's one of them—no mistake about it! If I only go cunningly I shall make my fortune. But they say a body must never take their eyes off one of them sort of creatures, not for a moment, or they'll surely escape.'

So Tom stole on to within arm's reach, just as a cat creeps up to a mouse, with his eye fixed on the little man.

'God bless your work, neighbour,' said Tom with his eyes fixed and his hand ready.

The little man raised up his head. 'Thank you kindly,' says he.

'I wonder you'd be working on the holiday!' says Tom.

'That's my business, not yours,' answers the little man.

'Maybe you'd be civil enough to tell what you've got in the pitcher there?' asks Tom.

'That I will,' says the tiny old man. 'It's good beer.'

'Beer!' says Tom. 'Thunder and fire! And where did you get it?'

'Where did I get it, is it you're asking? I made it. And what do you think I made it of?'

'The Deel knows,' says Tom. 'Malt and hops, I suppose, what else?'

'There you're out,' says the teeny weeny man, 'I made it of heather.'

'Of heather!' says Tom, bursting out laughing. 'Sure you don't think me such a fool as to believe that?'

'Do as you please,' answers the little man, 'but what I tell you is the truth. Did you never hear tell of the Danes?'

'Deed and I did, but what about *them*?' says Tom.

'Why, when those old Danes were here, they taught us to make beer out of heather, and the secret's in my family ever since.'

'Well, and isn't it the clever little fellow ye are! Will ye give me a taste of your beer?' says Tom.

But the little man looked angry at that. 'It would be fitter for you young man,' said he with a frown, 'to be looking after your father's property than to be bothering decent quiet bodies with foolish questions! Look yonder! Can't you see! There's the cows have broke into the oats, and are knocking it all about,' and with that the little thing pointed behind Tom's back.

Tom was taken so by surprise that he was just on the very point of looking round, just the way the little thing wanted. But instead he remembered in time, and he made a grab at the Lepracaun, and caught him up in his hand. But, oh dear! In his hurry Tom overturned the pitcher, and spilt all the heather beer, so that he never got a taste of it to tell what sort it was. The lad felt angry at that and said with an oath that he would kill the deceitful old fellow if he did not show him where his treasure was hidden, for, as Tom knew very well, such little folk always have a crock of gold buried in some hiding-place or another. Tom looked wicked as he spoke, and the little man seemed quite frightened; so says he:

'Come along then a couple of fields off, I suppose I'll have to show you where I've hid my gold.'

So Tom strode off, still holding the Lepracaun fast in his hand, and as they went, he never took his eyes off him, even though they had to cross hedges and ditches, and a crooked bit of bog. Well, at last they came to a great field full of boliauns, and the Lepracaun pointed to a big boliaun, and says he with a sigh:

'Dig under that boliaun, and you'll get the great crock! All full of guineas it is!'

Now Tom, in his hurry, had never thought of fetching a spade, so now what was he to do? He thought for a bit and then he made up his mind that there was nothing for it, but to run off home as fast as he could and get one; but, so that he might be sure to know the right place again, he took off one of his red garters, and he tied it fast round the boliaun. Then he said to the Lepracaun, and he spoke very suspicious like:

'Swear to me that you'll not take that garter away from that boliaun!'

The Lepracaun swore right away that, Faith, he wouldn't so much as touch it.

'I suppose,' ended up the Lepracaun, and he spoke very politely, 'you won't be needing me any more?'

'No,' says Tom at last, after he'd thought a bit more. 'You've sworn not to touch the mark I put on that boliaun to know it again, and so I don't see that I'll be needing you. Yes, you may go now. God speed you, and good luck attend you.'

'Good-bye to you then, Tom Fitzpatrick,' said the Lepracaun, 'and much good may my crock of gold do you when you get it,' and with that Tom set the little thing down and away it went.

As you can guess, Tom ran home for dear life, found a spade, and then back with it, as hard as he could go—back to the field of boliauns.

But, oh dear! When he got there, what did he see! It's true the Lepracaun hadn't touched the mark, but now there wasn't a boliaun in the whole big field but had a red garter, the very model of his own, tied fast around it!

What was Tom to do? To start digging up the whole field, that was all nonsense, for there were more than forty good Irish acres in it! Indeed, Tom soon saw that there was nothing for it, but to go home again with his spade on his shoulder, a little cooler than he went. Many's the hearty curse he gave to that Lepracaun every time he thought of the neat turn he had served him.

THE FAIRY CHILD

Once upon a time, but it wasn't in your time nor yet in mine, there lived a good woman named Margaret Huson, who earned her living by going out to nurse sick people, or to look after mother and child when a baby was born.

One night, it was at twelve o'clock and she had been long a-bed and asleep, there came a great knocking at her cottage door. Whoever it was that was knocking and shouting made such a noise that it quite frightened her. However, she put her head out of the window to ask what was the matter.

There was no moon and it was cloudy, and very dark, but she thought she could see a big horse tied out in the lane, and that it was a man who was standing on her doorstep and making all that racket—shouting and banging on the door with his riding whip.

When he saw her, he called up that it was his wife that needed her help, now at once, and that if she would make haste, she would be well paid.

So she lit her candle, dressed herself as fast as she could, and came down to him with a lantern. She opened the door, and then, for the first time, she saw his

face in the flickering light. He wasn't very tall, but he was very strange looking, squint-eyed, and indeed rather an ugly fellow. So little did she like his looks that she was almost for turning back and bolting the door in his face; but, as if he guessed her thoughts, he pressed a piece of gold money into her hand, telling her that she would be perfectly safe if she would come with him. So she said no more, slipped the gold piece into her pocket, locked her cottage door behind her, and went with him into the lane. A large coal black horse was waiting, and it seemed to the good woman that it had eyes like balls of fire. The queer-looking fellow seemed to know that she was hesitating again, and urged her on once more, saying that his wife needed her at once.

'Your wife, is it?' thought Mistress Huson. 'If she's anything like you, Heaven forgive me, but, sure as I live, I'm going to the birth of a black imp!'

However, without more ado, the old fellow whisked her up on to a high pillion and got up in front of her. Away they went, so fast that it seemed to her that they must be sailing through the air. She was so frightened that she shut her eyes and clung as tight as she could to the leather strap that the queer fellow wore round his waist. And so they thunderd along, full tilt, through a night that was as dark as that horse's black hide.

They stopped at last, and the good woman opened her eyes, and glad she was to be lifted down off that great black horse, and still more glad when she found herself in front of a neat cottage, and saw a couple of tidy children. She went inside, and found that her patient was a decent-looking young woman, that a nice fire was burning with a kettle singing on it, and that a cradle stood ready, as well as clothes and all other necessary things for the baby.

In due time a fine boy baby was born. Mistress Huson noticed nothing strange about it, except that it seemed very strong for its age. For instance, when Margaret Huson, as nurses usually do, was coaxing and cooing, and talking baby-talk to it, calling it a 'Pretty dear' and a 'Sweet pretty duck', and so on, and saying how like its *dear* father it was, the baby gave her a very old-fashioned look and a good box on the ear. The mother didn't seem surprised, so Mistress Huson thought it best to take no notice either.

Presently, when she had the little thing laid on her knees in front of the fire and had nearly finished washing it, the mother leant out from her bed and gave the nurse a small box of ointment and asked her to rub the child's eyes with it.

Now there seemed to be nothing wrong with the baby's eyes, so, although she did as she was told, the nurse wondered what this could be for.

'No doubt,' says she to herself, 'there's something good in it!' So she decided that she might just as well try a little of it herself. So she watched and, when the mother wasn't looking, she made free to rub one of her own eyes with the mysterious ointment.

Oh, what a change she saw. Everything was different The neat cottage, the mother in her bed, the tidy children—nothing was the same! Some things had changed for the better, some for the worse. She saw that she wasn't in a cottage at all but was sitting under the branches of an old oak, whose hollow and moss-grown trunk she had mistaken for the fireplace. Fire and candle were nothing but glow-worms; the new-made mother now seemed to be a most beautiful lady with long shining hair and was dressed in white silk, the baby

clothes were all made of a silky, silvery gauze, and the baby itself—although it had given her a box on the ear—looked much prettier than before, though it still had strange, slanting black eyes like its father. As for the good, tidy, clean children, where were they? Now she could see that they were two flat-nosed hairy imps that were busy climbing and tearing about, grinning and grimacing, and only sitting down now and then to scratch themselves, or to pull the beautiful lady's hair with their long, hairy paws.

It was all that the good woman could do to keep a quiet tongue, to finish her business as if nothing had happened, and to hand over the baby when she had dried and dressed it. However she managed it, even if her hands did tremble a little. When it was done, the sour-looking fellow was ready for her again. He lifted her up on to the coal-black horse as before, and, once more, he swung himself into the saddle in front of her, and then back they went, even faster than they had come.

How glad old Margaret Huson was to find that the day was beginning to break and that she was safe in her own cottage again!

Now whatever, or whoever, he might be, the squinty-eyed fellow had paid her well for her work. So on the next market-day she went out with a full purse to buy what she wanted. She hadn't been long among the market stalls when whom should she see but the very same queer-looking fellow that had stood at her door at midnight. And what do you think he was doing now? Why, he had a little wooden scraper in his hand, and he was going from stall to stall where such things as cheese and butter were put out, and was scraping a little off every cheese and every roll of butter, and putting it in little pots that hung by his side. And when he had got as much of these things as he wanted, he helped himself—

as cool as could be—to this and to that from off the other market stalls—meat, carrots, flour, cabbage, apples, and all the rest. Of course she expected that someone would be sure to call out 'Stop, thief!' but no one took any notice.

Now she felt a bit awkward about speaking to him (considering what he was up to) but presently, as he went round the stalls, he came quite near to her; so, feeling sure that he had noticed her, and seeing he had paid her so well, she plucked up courage, dropped him a curtsey, and said:

'Good-morning to you, sir! And how is your lady and the fine little baby?'

'What!' says he, turning round very quick. 'Do you see me today?'

'See you,' says she, 'to be sure I do, as plain as I see the sun in the sky. And I can see you're busy too!' And she pursed up her lips.

'You do, do you!' says he. 'And pray, with which eye do you see all this?'

'With the right eye, to be sure,' says she, quite proud to have caught him out.

'The ointment! The ointment!' he shrieked. 'Take that for meddling with what didn't belong to you!' And with that he struck her on the right eye and vanished.

And from that day, till the day she died, Margaret Huson was blind in her right eye.

MR. MIACCA

Tommy Grimes was sometimes a good boy, and sometimes a bad boy; and when he was a bad boy, he was a very bad boy. His mother used to say to him:

'Tommy, Tommy, be a good boy, and don't go out of our street, or else Mr. Miacca will have you.'

But still, on the days when he was a bad boy, he would go out of the street. One day, sure enough, he had scarcely got round the corner, when Mr. Miacca caught him and popped him into a bag, upside down, and took him off to his house.

When Mr. Miacca got Tommy inside the house, he pulled him out of the bag and set him down, and felt his arms and legs.

'You're rather tough,' says he, 'but you're all I've got for supper, and you'll not taste bad boiled. But body o' me, I've forgot the herbs, and it's bitter you'll taste without herbs. Sally! Here, I say, Sally!' And he called Mrs. Miacca.

So Mrs. Miacca came out of another room and said: 'What d'ye want, my dear?'

'Oh, here's a little boy for supper,' said Mr. Miacca,

'but I've forgot the herbs. Mind him, will ye, while I go for them.'

'All right, my love,' says Mrs. Miacca, and off he goes. Then Tommy Grimes said to Mrs. Miacca:

'Does Mr. Miacca always have little boys for supper?'

'Mostly, my dear,' said Mrs. Miacca, 'if little boys are bad enough, and come his way.'

'And don't you have anything else but boy-meat? No pudding?' asked Tommy.

'Ah, I loves pudding,' says Mrs. Miacca. 'But it's not often the likes of us gets pudding.'

'Why, my mother is making a pudding this very day,' said Tommy Grimes, 'and I am sure she'd give you some, if I asked her. Shall I run and get some?'

'Now, that's a thoughtful boy,' said Mrs. Miacca, 'only don't be long and be sure to be back in time for supper.'

So off Tommy peltered, and right glad he was to get off so cheap; and for many a long day he was as good as good could be, and never went round the corner out of the street.

But, somehow, he couldn't always remember to be good; and one day he went round the corner again, and as luck would have it, he hadn't scarcely got round it when Mr. Miacca grabbed him up, popped him in his bag, and took him home.

When he got him there, Mr. Miacca dropped him out; and when he saw who it was, he said:

'Ah, you're the youngster that served me and my missus such a shabby trick, leaving us without any supper! Well, you shan't do it again. I'll watch over you myself. Here, get under the sofa, and I'll sit on it and watch the pot boil for you.'

So poor Tommy Grimes had to creep under the sofa, and Mr. Miacca sat on it and waited for the pot to boil. And they waited, and they waited, but still the pot didn't boil, till at last Mr. Miacca got tired of waiting, and he said:

'Here, you under there, I'm not going to wait any longer. Put out your leg, and I'll stop your giving us the slip.'

So Tommy put out a leg, and Mr. Miacca got a chopper, and chopped it off, and popped it in the pot. Suddenly he calls out:

'Sally, my dear! Sally!' and nobody answered. So he went into the next room to look for Mrs. Miacca, and while he was there, Tommy crept out from under the sofa and ran out of the door. For you see, it wasn't his own leg, but the leg of the sofa that he had put out.

So Tommy Grimes ran home, and he never went round the corner again till he was old enough to go alone.

THE SECRET ROOM

Once upon a time there lived a mother with three daughters. The job the girls had was to guard the cabbage-patch in front of the cottage. One day they were all sitting in the sun spinning, when what should they see but a bull in the cabbage-patch.

'Take your distaff and run, child, run!' said the mother to the eldest daughter.

So the girl took her distaff and ran. The bull ran and she ran, and she ran and the bull ran, until they came to a house at the edge of a wood. There the bull gave her a large bunch of keys, and told her that she could go anywhere in the house she liked except one room. He showed her the key to this room, and told her that she mustn't unlock the door to which it belonged. Then the bull went away and left her. The girl took the keys and roamed from one beautiful room to another, until she had seen them all except the forbidden room. But this was the one she most wanted to see.

At last she couldn't bear not knowing what was in it, so what did she do, but she opened the door and went inside. But, oh dear! The room was full of headless bodies which hung against all the walls. She locked the door and ran downstairs, but when she looked, she saw that there was blood on the key, on her hand, and on her shoes. As she was trying the best she knew how to get the blood off, along came a big black cat, which said to her:

'Mew, mew, mew! Give me a dish of bread and milk and I will tell you how to get the blood off.'

'Go away, you black old thing!' says she. 'I'm not going to bother with you.'

So the cat went away, and pretty soon the bull came.

'Let me see your keys!' said he. 'How came the blood on this one?'

Then he asked to see her hands and her shoes. When he saw blood on them too, he knew that she had disobeyed him; so he cut her head off and hung her body up with all the others who had done the same.

The next day the mother and the two younger daughters again sat spinning in the sun, and again they saw the bull in the cabbage-patch. The mother sent the second daughter just as she had sent the first.

'Take your distaff and run child, run!' says she. But exactly the same things happened to her and she couldn't wash off the blood.

The third day it was only the mother and the youngest daughter who sat spinning. Again the mother looked up and saw the bull in the cabbage-patch.

'Take your distaff and run, child, run!' cried she just as she had done before.

So the youngest daughter ran and the bull ran. The bull ran and she ran, until they came to the great house at the edge of the wood. There the bull gave her a bunch of keys, and told her that she might open every

door in the house except the one whose key he showed her. Then the bull went away. The youngest daughter did just as her two sisters had done, and went into all the rooms except the forbidden one. But she too kept wondering what could be in there, until her curiosity got to be more than she could bear, so that she unlocked the door and went in. She was so horrified by what she saw that she quickly shut the door and ran downstairs, but with the tell-tale blood on the key, on her hand, and on her shoes.

To her came the big black cat, who said:

'Mew, mew, mew! Give me a dish of bread and milk, and I will tell you how to get the blood off.'

Instead of telling the cat to go away, as her two sisters had done, she went and got him some bread and milk.

When the cat had finished eating, he said:

'Go into the attic and you will find a sickle. Take it, rub it on the key, on your hand, and on your shoes, while you say, "Blood, be gone! Blood, be gone!" '

The girl went to the attic, found the sickle, and did just as the cat had told her, saying, 'Blood, be gone! Blood, be gone!' Then she went downstairs, where she found the bull waiting for her.

'Let me see your keys,' he said, 'and your hands and your shoes!'

When he saw that she had no bloodstains upon her, he suddenly changed from a bull into a beautiful prince.

'I was bewitched,' he said, 'by a girl who first loved me and then hated me because I wouldn't marry her. I killed many a girl while I was a bull, but now we will have the bodies taken care of, and then we will be married.'

Married they were, and lived happily ever after.

WHITE-FACED SIMMINY

In olden times, when a girl wanted a place as a servant, off she would go to a hiring-fair.

Well, one day, there was a young farm-girl who wanted a place, and so off she went to the fair like the rest. She stood with the others and each one had a posy of flowers to show that they were all seeking a new place.

One girl was hired and another was hired, but there she stood. At last, towards evening, a funny-looking little old man came along, hired the farm-girl, and off they went to his house.

He seemed a nice old fellow, and they had supper together. Afterwards, while they were sitting before the fire, he told her that in his house he expected the servant always to call things by their proper names.

'What would you call *me*, for instance?' says he.

'Master, or Mister, or whatever you please, Sir,' said she.

'No,' says he, 'you must call me Don Nippery Septo. And what would you call these?' says he, pointing to his shoes.

'Slippers, or shoes, or whatever you please, Sir.'

'You must call them Hay-down-treaders, my dear. And what would you call these?' and he pointed to his trousers.

'Breeches or bags, or whatever you please, Sir.'

'No, you must call them Fortune's Crackers. And what's this?' says he, pointing to the staircase.

'Steps or stairs, or whatever you please, Sir.'

'Not a bit of it, my girl! That's the Wooden Hill, and up there is my Barnacle,' he said, pointing to where his bed was, up above. 'And what would you call her now?' asked he, as he stroked the cat.

'Cat, or Kit, or whatever you please, Sir.'

'No, no! You must call her White-faced Simminy. And this here,' and he pointed to the fire.

'Fire, or heat, or whatever you please, Sir.'

'Dear me no! It's Hot Cockolorum. And what is *this*?' and he showed her what was in a bucket.

'Water, or wet, or whatever you please, Sir.'

'Not at all! That's Pondolorum. And what would you call this?' said he, pointing to the house.

'Cottage, or house, or whatever you please, Sir.'

'No! No! Great Castle of Strawbungle, is its name.'

That very night the girl, in a fright, woke up her master and this is what she said:

'Don Nippery Septo! Get out of your barnacle and put on your hay-down-treaders and your fortune's crackers, and come down the wooden hill as fast as you can. For White-faced Simminy has got a spark of hot cockolorum on her tail and unless you get some more pondolorum, the Great Castle of Strawbungle will soon be all on hot cockolorum.'

JACK AND THE BEANSTALK

Once upon a time there was a poor widow who had an only son called Jack. Jack was one who liked playing better than work, I agree, but all the same you couldn't say he was a bad lad. Indeed he was a very good-natured boy and fond of his mother.

The only thing they had to live on was selling the milk of their white cow, but at last there came a time when the white cow didn't give any more milk and the poor widow was very miserable and sat wringing her hands.

'What shall we do? What shall we do?' said she.

'Cheer up, Mother! I'll go and get work somewhere,' said Jack.

'We've tried that! But everybody knows what an idle boy you are! *You'd* be the last to get a job,' said his mother. 'We'd better sell the cow and then we could use the money to start a stall in the market.'

Now the next day happened to be market-day and so his mother got the cow ready, gave the halter into Jack's hand and told him to get the best price he could for her.

He hadn't gone far when he met an old woman, all dressed in rags, who greeted him kindly.

'Good morning, Jack,' says the old woman.

'Good morning to you,' says Jack, and he wondered how it was she knew his name.

'Where are you off to?' asked the old woman.

'I'm off to the market to sell our cow,' he told her.

'What do you know about selling cows?' said the old woman. 'I don't believe you know how many beans make five.'

'Yes, I do,' Jack told her, 'two in each hand and one in your mouth.'

'Quite right,' said the old woman, 'and here are the very beans.' With that she put her hand into her pocket and pulled out five very strange-looking beans, each one a different colour.

Jack thought them very pretty.

'If you like them so well, I'll give you these beans in exchange for your cow,' said the old woman.

Jack shook his head.

'Ah, but you don't know what sort these beans are,' she said. 'If you plant them at night, by next morning they'll have grown right up to the sky.'

'Right up to the sky?' said Jack in surprise.

'Yes, that's right,' she answered, 'and if they don't grow as I say you can have your cow back.'

'Done!' says Jack, and with that he hands over the cow's halter and puts the beans in his pocket.

Now he hadn't got very far from home when he met the old woman, so it didn't take him long going back. His mother was surprised to see him home again so soon.

'Back already, Jack?' says she. 'I see you haven't got the cow so you must have sold her. How much did you get?'

'You'll never guess,' says Jack. ''Twasn't money at all.'

'Not money?' says she. 'Well, what did you get?'

So now Jack pulled out the pretty beans.

'They're magic beans,' he told her. 'Plant them overnight and next morning——'

'Magic indeed!' says his mother in a fury. 'You fool, you dolt! You idiot!' and with that the poor woman burst into tears. 'The last thing we had to sell! Our good cow! The best milker in the parish. Oh Jack, what have you done! We're ruined,' and with that, in her despair, his mother snatched the beans out of Jack's hand and threw them out of the window. Then she told Jack to get away out of her sight.

Well, Jack didn't say much, in fact he went off to his bed. For the more he thought about it, the more he thought he'd been silly, and the more sorry he was that his mother should have been so disappointed. He was hungry too, for his mother had been too cross to give him anything to eat. All the same he dropped off to sleep at last.

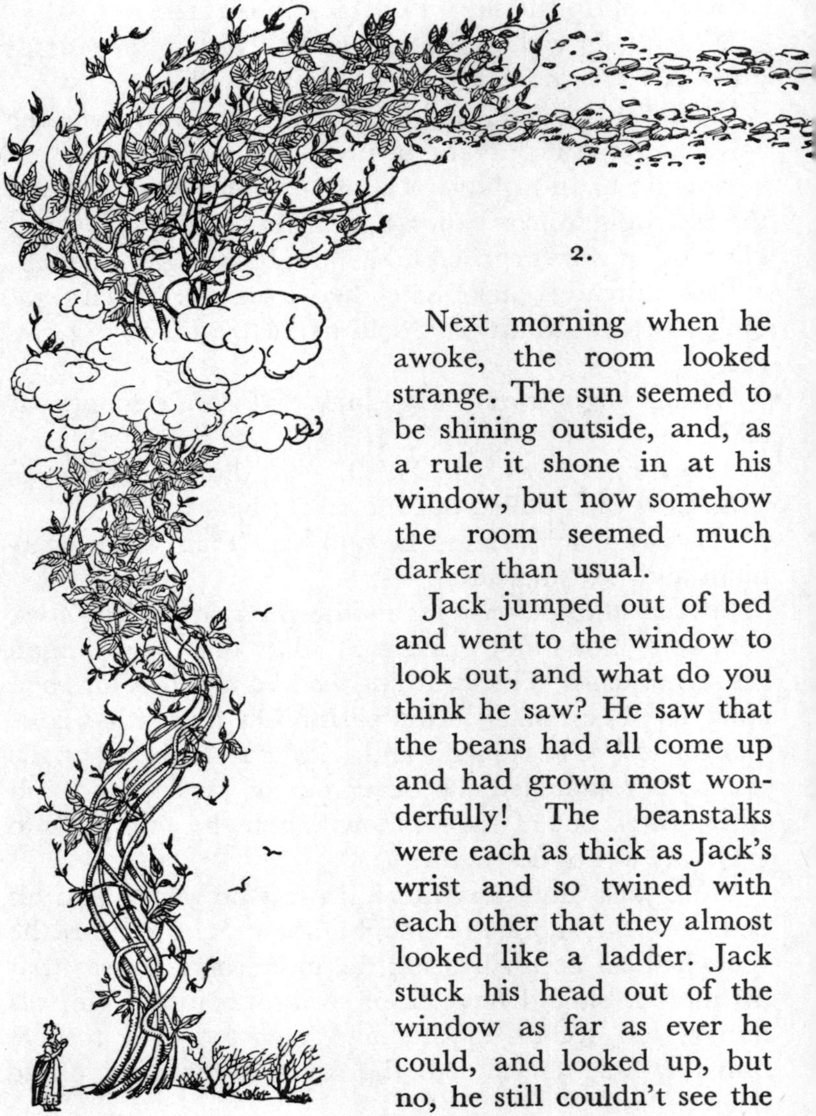

2.

Next morning when he awoke, the room looked strange. The sun seemed to be shining outside, and, as a rule it shone in at his window, but now somehow the room seemed much darker than usual.

Jack jumped out of bed and went to the window to look out, and what do you think he saw? He saw that the beans had all come up and had grown most wonderfully! The beanstalks were each as thick as Jack's wrist and so twined with each other that they almost looked like a ladder. Jack stuck his head out of the window as far as ever he could, and looked up, but no, he still couldn't see the top.

He dressed himself as quickly as he could and went outside. There were the beanstalks climbing right up into the sky, and *still*, even now, he couldn't see the top of them.

His mother soon came out as well and she was quite as much surprised as Jack, but she was frightened as well. When Jack said he was going to climb up and see where the beanstalks went to, she begged him not to go. But as you can guess, she begged in vain. Jack simply had to find out, and setting his foot on the strong twining stalks he was soon out of sight.

He climbed, and he climbed, and he climbed, and he *climbed*, higher, higher, and yet higher, till his arms and legs ached, till the clouds rolled below him. But still the beanstalk went higher. At last he found that he had got to level ground, and that he was in a strange new country.

Jack could not see any houses, or bushes, or trees or any living creatures either; nothing but rough stones lying about all round. However, he began to walk along a straight rough sort of road, when whom should he see, but the very same old woman who had given him the beans.

'Are you sorry you made that bargain with me?' says she.

'That's as may be,' says Jack, scratching his head. 'It depends what I find here!'

'Did you ever hear tell about your father, Jack?' says she.

'No, or but very little,' said Jack. 'But what's that got to do with it?'

'Sit down,' says the old woman, 'and I'll tell you.' Then she told him something that his mother had never told him. A wicked Ogre had killed his father and had carried away everything he owned. The Ogre had done this because Jack's father was a good man and had shared his money with those who had nothing. Jack had been a baby when all this happened and the Ogre had threatened his mother that if ever she told anybody, he would come down and eat them both for breakfast.

'Where's this Ogre?' said Jack, clenching his fists. The old woman just pointed down the long rough road, but before she vanished, she told him what he must do.

So Jack went on alone along the rough straight road, and a long way it was. However, after a while, he saw in

the distance a great tall house, and when he came to it, he saw a great tall woman on the doorstep.

'Good evening,' says Jack, very politely. 'Could you be so kind as to give me some supper?' (He had not had anything to eat, you know, the night before and no breakfast either, so he was as hungry as a hunter.)

'It's supper you want?' said the great tall woman, shaking her head. 'No, no! It's supper you'll be if you don't move off from here. My husband is an Ogre and there is nothing he likes better than grilled boy on toast.'

'Oh, please,' cried Jack, 'do give me something to eat. I've had nothing since yesterday morning, and I may as well be grilled as die of hunger!'

Well, after a while the Ogre's wife agreed, for she felt quite sorry for Jack. So she took him into the kitchen and gave him a hunk of bread, some cheese and a jug of milk.

But Jack hadn't half finished when thump, thump, thump, the whole house began to tremble.

'Goodness me! It's my old man!' said the Ogre's wife. 'Come along quick, and jump in here!' and she bundled Jack into the oven just as the Ogre came in.

He was as big an Ogre as ever you saw. He had three young calves strung up by the heels hanging from his belt and he unslung them all and said to his wife:

'Here, wife, broil me a couple of these for supper!' But then he began to sniff about.

'Fee-fi-fo-fum,
I smell the blood of an Englishman.
Be he alive, or be he dead
I'll grind his bones to spice my bread.'

Well, his wife told him not to talk nonsense. She made out that he was dreaming and she began to get ready the calves for his supper. As she went about her work she passed the oven, peeped in and whispered to Jack, who was in a sore fright and just going to jump out:

'Wait till he is asleep. He always has a sleep after supper.'

Well, presently, supper was ready and the Ogre sat down to it. After he had finished he went to a big chest and took out a bag of gold and began to count it. At last his head began to nod and he began to snore until the whole house shook again.

When he heard that noise, Jack crept out of his oven and when he was passing the Ogre he reached up on tiptoe, got hold of the bag that was still half full of gold, slung it on his back as well as he could, and off he went, helter skelter, as fast as his legs could carry him, down the rough straight road.

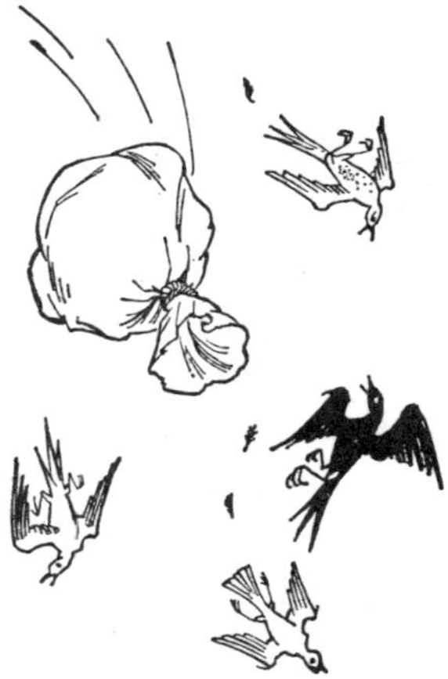

At last he got to where the top of the beanstalk came up. He could only see cloud down below, but he threw the bag of gold down and luckily it fell into his mother's garden. Then down climbed Jack after it, and a long climb it was. However, at last he got home, told his mother his adventures, and showed her the gold.

As you can guess his mother was very much frightened to hear how he had found out about his father's death and was terrified that the Ogre would come down after them. However, after a while she cheered up. There was the gold and they were able to live well now.

But Jack couldn't rest. He wanted to go up the beanstalk again. He wanted to see if he couldn't get something more and do a bit more to revenge his father's death. He made up his mind that, this time, he would disguise himself, and so he did. He disguised himself so well that when he had gone the length of the broad rough road and got to the great tall house, the great tall woman who was the Ogre's wife didn't recognize him.

'Good-morning, Ma'am,' says Jack. 'Could you be so good as to give me something to eat?'

'Go away, boy,' says the big tall woman, 'or else my man will eat you for breakfast.'

Well, Jack wasn't taking no for an answer. At first she wouldn't let him come in, but at last he begged so hard she let him in, and, once more, put bread and cheese and milk in front of him. But he had not eaten the half of it when, just as before, thump, thump, thump, they heard the Ogre's footsteps and the Ogre's wife again hid Jack in the oven.

Once more the Ogre thought he smelt a human, once more his wife told him that he was dreaming. This time it was not calves, but oxen, that he had brought home for her to cook for him and the smell of roast beef soon filled the kitchen.

When breakfast was done and he had finished eating, he said:

'Wife, bring in the hen that lays the golden eggs.' So she brought in the hen. Jack was peeping from out of the oven. The Ogre said, 'Lay', and Jack saw the hen lay a bright golden egg that shone in the light.

Well, the Ogre amused himself like that for a while, and then again once more he fell asleep. Again Jack waited till he snored so loud that the house shook. Then Jack crept out of his oven, picked up the magic hen and was off before you could say, 'Knife!'

But oh dear! Just as he was going out of the door the hen gave a loud cackle. Jack's heart almost stood still. However, the Ogre did not quite wake up properly; he just called out:

'Wife, wife, what are you doing to my hen?'

Well, as you can guess, Jack didn't wait to hear the answer to *that* question. Off he ran along the long straight road, got to the beanstalk and down he climbed as fast as ever he could.

When he got home he showed his mother the wonderful hen and whenever he said, 'Lay' to it, it laid a golden egg just as it had done for the Ogre.

3.

Now you may think that Jack would have been content with this, but he was not! He hated the Ogre, and besides he was sure there must be more treasure in that great tall house.

So one morning, without a word to his mother, he got up early. So she shouldn't hear him, he climbed out of his bedroom window straight on to the beanstalk. Once more he climbed and he climbed, and he climbed, until at last he got to the top, and he saw the broad straight road. But this time he didn't go directly to the Ogre's house. When he got near it, he waited behind a big rock until he saw the great tall woman come out of the house with a huge pail in her hands and go down to the stream to fetch water. Then, when her back was turned, he slipped in at the door and hid himself, not in the oven this time, but in the copper.

He hadn't been there long when once more the Ogre came in and soon afterwards his wife as well, with the buckets of water that were as big as cottages. The Ogre began to sniff round.

'Fee-fi-fo-fum,
I smell the blood of an Englishman.
Be he alive, or be he dead,
I'll grind his bones to spice my bread.'

'I smell him, I really do smell him, wife!' cried the Ogre.

'Do you, dearie?' said his wife. 'These boys really are a dreadful nuisance. I'll never forget how one stole your gold, and then another your hen. Well, if it is one of *those* boys, he's sure to have got into the oven!'

So they both went over to look in the oven, but luckily, that was not where Jack was. They looked in a few other places, but soon the Ogre's wife got tired of it.

'There you are again with your "Fee-fi-fo-fum",' said she. 'Of course there isn't anything!'

So, after hunting a bit more, the Ogre agreed to have his meal and down he sat. But he still didn't feel sure, so every now and again he would lay down his knife and fork and search in the larder and the cupboards. Luckily for Jack he never thought of the copper. After he had finished eating, he called out:

'Wife, wife, bring me my golden harp,' and she brought it, and it shone so bright that the whole room was lit up by it, and when the giant said, 'Sing', the harp sang most beautifully until at last the giant went to sleep.

When he began to snore Jack lifted up the copper lid very quietly, then out he crept on hands and knees. He crept, and he crept, till he had crawled up to the table. Then he reached up on tip-toe, got hold of the golden harp, and rushed with it towards the door, as fast as his legs would carry him.

But the harp called out, quite loud:

'Master! Master!'

And this time the Ogre jumped up, wide-awake, and just caught sight of Jack whisking round the door with the glittering harp.

As you can guess, Jack ran as he had never run before, and the Ogre ran after him, and Jack would certainly have been caught, if he hadn't had a start and if he hadn't dodged a bit.

By the time Jack got to the top of the beanstalk the Ogre was not many of his great long steps behind him, but what was the Ogre's surprise when he saw Jack disappear. Peering down, he saw Jack underneath, legging it down and down the beanstalk, climbing down for dear life.

Well then, the Ogre didn't know quite what to do, and stood there puzzled. But the golden harp in Jack's arms cried up to him:

'Master! Master!'

When he heard it, the Ogre swung himself down off the ground and on to the beanstalk, which as you can guess, fairly shook underneath his huge weight.

Down climbed Jack, faster and faster and after him came the Ogre, and all the while Jack was shouting to his mother:

'Mother! Mother! Quick! Quick! Bring the axe. Bring the axe!'

Luckily his mother heard him, and she came rushing out of the house with the axe in her hand, but when she got to the beanstalk she stood still with fright, for there, quite plainly, she saw the Ogre's huge legs and feet, just coming down through the clouds.

At that very moment Jack jumped down to earth, took the axe, and gave such a chop to the beanstalk that it was nearly cut in two. The Ogre felt the beanstalk quiver. Another blow with the axe and the beanstalk came clean in two. Down fell the beanstalk and the Ogre with it, and as luck would have it he fell bang on his head and broke his neck, and the beanstalk came down on the top of him. So that was the end both of beanstalk and Ogre.

But what with the hen that laid the golden eggs and the glittering harp that sang sweetly whenever they liked, Jack and his mother were rich and happy, and Jack married a beautiful princess, and they all lived happily ever after.